Christopher Marlowe

Thomas Healy

Northcote House
in association with
The British Council

In memory of

John Norton-Smith
1931–1988

First published in 1994 by Northcote House Publishers Ltd, Plymbridge House,
Estover Road, Plymouth PL6 7PZ, United Kingdom.
Tel: (0752) 735251. Fax: (0752) 695699. Telex: 45635.

British Library Cataloguing-in-Publication Data
A catalogue record for this book is available from the British Library

ISBN 0 7463 0707 1

Typeset by Kestrel Data, Exeter
Printed and bound in the United Kingdom by BPC Wheatons Ltd, Exeter

Contents

Biographical Outline

The dating of Marlowe's plays and poems is uncertain. I have given the first date for which clear evidence exists to support claims for performances or editions.

1564	Christopher Marlowe born at Canterbury. His father, John, is a shoemaker.
1578/9	Enters the King's School, Canterbury, as a scholar. Prior to this he was probably educated at small private schools in Canterbury.
1580/1	Enters Corpus Christi College, Cambridge, on a scholarship recently established by Matthew Parker, Archbishop of Canterbury.
1584	Receives his BA.
1584–7	Absent from Cambridge for long periods, apparently working as an undercover agent for the Government.
1587	Receives his MA.
1587–93	Active as a dramatist in London. Continues to work as an undercover agent.
1587/8	*Tamburlaine* acted.
1590	*Tamburlaine* first published.
1591	Begins sharing writing chambers with the dramatist Thomas Kyd.
1591/2	*The Jew of Malta* acted.
1593	*The Massacre at Paris* acted.
1593	(12 May) Kyd arrested on suspicion of libel. His and Marlowe's rooms are searched, and ostensibly heretical papers are discovered, which Kyd claims belong to Marlowe.
1593	(20 May) Instructed by Privy Council to report to it daily.
1593	(30 May) Killed by Ingram Frizer in a Deptford eating house during an argument about paying the bill. Frizer's claim of self-defence is accepted by authorities and he is pardoned on 28 June.
1593	(1 June) Privy Council receives a statement from Richard Baines, who worked in espionage, proclaiming Marlowe as a heretic.
1594	*Doctor Faustus* acted. *Edward II* and *Dido, Queen of Carthage* first published.
1598	*Hero and Leander* first published.
1603	*The Massacre at Paris* published by this date.
1604	The 'A version' of *Doctor Faustus* published.
1616	The 'B version' of *Doctor Faustus* published.
1633	*The Jew of Malta* published.

Preface

This is a book about Marlowe's drama. While not adopting a single critical perspective from which to approach these plays, it will be clear that I am fascinated by them as representations of an Elizabethan culture we increasingly find less uniform and less easily categorized than we previously thought. We know little of Marlowe as a writer and I do not try to link his works in an intimate manner with our sketchy knowledge of his life. My interest in him is principally as a cultural agent, a participant in the preoccupations, beliefs, and anxieties found in Elizabethan society – ones which continue to pose challenging questions for our current cultural environments. Although the book is divided into sections which often focus on one play, I have resisted a methodical play-by-play study.

David Bevington's and Eric Rasmussen's recent scholarly edition of *Doctor Faustus* prints two different versions of the play and proposes the author as 'Christopher Marlowe and his collaborator and revisers'. This illustrates the dilemmas we face both in trying to pin-point a single intelligence behind Marlowe's works and in selecting the plays' most reliable editions. The particular status of Marlowe's texts makes it more difficult than usual for the critical writer to choose an edition from which to draw quotations. The standard scholarly edition of the plays is an expensive two-volume hardback many readers are unlikely to have access to. Using either it or editions of single plays would make it difficult for students to refer to the sections of the works I discuss because there is no agreement on how Marlowe's plays should be divided into acts or scenes. For convenience, therefore, I have opted to quote Marlowe from J. B. Steane's one-volume modern spelling edition of *The Complete Plays*. This is the volume I find remains in widest circulation with readers, but I would strongly recommend anyone seriously interested in Marlowe to consult either Fredson Bowers's or C. F. Tucker Brooke's old-spelling editions (details may be found in the bibliography at the end).

In keeping with the policy of Writers and their Work, I have been sparing with references and avoided notes. Spelling in original documents cited has not been modernized beyond the usual conventions of transforming 'v' to 'u', 'i' to 'j', and so forth. For those who would also like to examine Marlowe's poetry, which (notably *Hero and Leander*) repays acquaintance, the bibliography includes suggestions for study.

Acknowledgements

I have always wanted an opportunity to write on Marlowe and owe much to Isobel Armstrong for the invitation to attempt this book, providing me with just the excuse (if one was needed) to spend a year working on the plays. I am extremely grateful to my colleagues in the English Department at Birkbeck College for allowing me a light teaching year in which to accomplish the reading and writing for this project. Though the study was undertaken in a relatively short space of time, I have managed to subject a considerable number of people to many of my ideas and have been privileged to benefit from the advice of some excellent Marlovians. Richard Wilson offered me many fruits from his exciting research, as well as the opportunity of speaking at Lancaster. Martin Hilsky at Prague, Javier Sanchez at SEDERI in Las Palmas, Darryl Grantly at Kent, and Gordon Campbell at ESSE in Bordeaux also extended invitations to speak and provided forums where some of this book's arguments could be tested. Tony Parr and Alan Stewart allowed me to read as yet unpublished research from which I learnt much. Kenneth Parker, Gareth Roberts, Alexander Shurbanov, Alan Sinfield, and Thomas Sorge offered stimulating conversation. Margaret Healy and Boika Sokolova read drafts of the manuscript, offering searching criticism and advice.

I properly began to appreciate the excitement and the difficulties of Marlowe's drama over a decade ago through discussions with John Norton-Smith. In many respects, Norton was a truly Marlovian character; he was certainly a shrewd student of the plays and was completing an edition of *Faustus* at his untimely death. I know this book would be a better one if he was still here.

Abbreviations

Dido	*Dido, Queen of Carthage*
Ed. II	*Edward the Second*
Faust.	*The Tragical History of Doctor Faustus*
Jew	*The Jew of Malta*
Massacre	*The Massacre at Paris*
1 Tamb.	*The First Part of Tamburlaine the Great*
2 Tamb.	*The Second Part of Tamburlaine the Great*

1

The Marlowe Effect

Christopher Marlowe's plays present pursuits of power and passion, they reveal deception and destructiveness, and they dwell on obsession. Marlowe's drama also presents farce and comic deflation of events – comedy and tragedy freely and often bizarrely mix, counter, or accommodate each other. Marlowe excels in extravagance of language and action, creating a poetry and drama of excess unmatched by any other British poet or playwright. In the seven plays he wrote (taking *Tamburlaine* as two distinct works) we witness among other incidents: the brutal torture and murder of an English king; a man dragged off to hell; an emperor and his wife dashing their brains out against prison bars; the suicide of a queen, her sister, and lover (and the queen's immolation); the killing of a daughter and a son by their parents; practical jokes played on a pope; massacres of Protestants, virgins, and various other groups; the betrayal of a king by his queen; apparitions of Helen of Troy and Alexander the Great; passionate homo- and heterosexual affairs. Such incidents have the potential merely to be gratuitous and collapse into pornography. Instead, Marlowe's spectacle is always designed to provoke, to unsettle, and to challenge. For all his recourse to embellished poetic language and a packed sequence of happenings in his plays, he is a writer of powerful ideas. He is able to match extravagance of action with a language which defies convention, questioning relations between word, action, and the structures for understanding the world which language fashions.

As a dramatic poet, Marlowe has an ability to paint in words. He can evoke scenes, histories, and emotional states which in their linguistic exaggeration confront readers' and audiences' preconceptions of reality. Extravagance is Marlowe's tool for an intellectual exploration of humanity's inability to live content in this world. His philosophy is scepticism, not in a cynical dismissive sense, but a recognition that the principles which govern the world remain obscure. Deception figures strongly in all his work – characters are

1

duped by others, they self-deceive or the audience is deceived. Nothing is what it seems to be. Humanity's attempt to negotiate the world largely appears for Marlowe a type of black comic-tragedy and his work is centred on those liminal moments where comic obsessions shift to tragic destructiveness.

Within the tragic, Marlowe discovers much entertainment. If, for Shakespeare, all the world is a stage where characters have parts which must be played, for Marlowe all the world is a circus. His theatre of excess is one where playing roles as extravagantly as possible often appears the desired end. His characters love theatricality for the showmanship. Where Shakespeare has Hamlet or Prospero wanting to be directors of productions which will force their players into some type of moral awareness, Marlowe's show-men love their dramas for the colour, daring, and roles they can give themselves – Tamburlaine with his tents draped in white, red, and black before Damascus; Faustus conjuring Helen for the scholars; the Jew of Malta arranging a catalogue of ingenious deaths. The need to create theatre is something Marlowe's writings continuously demonstrate. This desire for play is often recognized as unsustainable – as with Edward II's insistence on staging entertainments as his kingdom crumbles or Faustus's organized spectacles for emperor or nobles before his twenty-four-year pact with Lucifer elapses and he goes to hell – but it is none the less compelling. Where Milton in *Lycidas* found the prospect of an immortal poetic Fame the spur to 'scorn delights, and live laborious days', Marlowe proposes that a desire for worldly power and notoriety is a more powerful motivation to action. Dido readily contemplates her city Carthage being sacked as a second Troy if she can become a second Helen and Aeneas will play Paris. The Guise will gain the crown of France or 'rend it with my nails to naught' (*Massacre*, I. ii. 45). Barabas, the Jew of Malta, dies boiling in a cauldron intent that before the 'intolerable pangs' of the heat destroy him he will be able to reveal his murders and deceptions – 'Die life! fly soul! tongue, curse thy fill, and die!' (*Jew*, V. v. 94). There is no compromise in Marlowe's drama.

This extravagance forms the Marlowe effect; how it operates can be illustrated through considering three examples. Marlowe's writing creates a poetic richness from the decorous and ornamented models of eloquence which Renaissance culture promoted. He is particularly well versed in classical literature. As the Classics provided the staple diet of texts through which Elizabethan schools and universities

2

taught grammar, rhetoric, logic, and oratory (subjects which virtually constituted the entire curriculum), this is not surprising. Marlowe, though, used the Classics much more inventively than most of his contemporaries, and his dramatic characters constantly employ classical allusion to give themselves roles and desired identities – even the Jew of Malta proposes a revealing analogy to himself and his daughter in Agamemnon and Iphigenia. Articulating a poetic eloquence in dramatic contexts where it is conventionally unexpected is one of the most marked features of the Marlowe effect. He bridges what, initially, may seem a gap between language and action, confronting his reader or audience with a relation between the two that disturbs because it entices compliance in its displays of controlled exaggeration. The ability of this lyrical eloquence to allure aesthetically, shifting readers or audiences out of preconceived senses of moral, social, or religious orders, is one of this writing's most remarkable features. It allows dramatic actions to be witnessed in manners different from the ways we might normally be disposed to witness them, promoting a language in action which confronts many of the usual conventions within the Elizabethan world.

The first illustration of the Marlowe effect is from the first *Tamburlaine* play. Tamburlaine explains to the mortally wounded King of Persia why he has pursued his overthrow:

> The thirst of reign and sweetness of a crown,
> That caused the eldest son of heavenly Ops
> To thrust his doting father from his chair
> And place himself in th' empyreal heaven,
> Moved me to manage arms against thy state.
> What better precedent than mighty Jove?
> Nature, that framed us of four elements
> Warring within our breasts for regiment,
> Doth teach us all to have aspiring minds:
> Our souls, whose faculties can comprehend
> The wondrous architecture of the world
> And measure every wand'ring planet's course,
> Still climbing after knowledge infinite
> And always moving as the restless spheres,
> Wills us to wear ourselves and never rest
> Until we reach the ripest fruit of all,
> That perfect bliss and sole felicity,
> The sweet fruition of an earthly crown.

1 Tamb. II. vii. 12–29

Tamburlaine is a Scythian shepherd and one of the uncompromising features of Marlowe's plays about him is that he speaks so eloquently. For the Elizabethans, language was an indication of social standing: to be able to speak well ostensibly demonstrated nobility of blood. In Spenser's *Faerie Queene* or Sir Philip Sidney's *Arcadia*, for example, rustic figures who speak eloquently inevitably turn out to be disguised aristocracy or abandoned aristocrats who have been raised in rural surroundings (Cymbeline's sons in Shakespeare are another example). But Marlowe's Tamburlaine is genuinely of base parentage.

If Tamburlaine's capacity for eloquence is surprising, the speech is also disturbing. The apparent drift of the logic and the philosophical ideals which arise in its latter half would have been commonplace to a late-sixteenth-century audience. It was precisely humanity's capacity to use reason which separated people from beasts. The expected conclusion of this logic, however, would certainly have been a heavenly and not an earthly crown. Human aspiration was designed to be directed towards immortal life hereafter. The religious justification for human reason, and hence our use of the things of this world, was that it enabled humanity to gain a greater intimation of God through being able to discern the divine in nature. Tamburlaine substitutes a wholly worldly end – the earthly crown with its promises of material wealth and the exercise of power.

Tamburlaine having, therefore, apparently travestied the nature of human aspiration, and what conclusions eloquent language should reach, the play might subsequently be expected to perform his nemesis and decline into self-destructive tyranny. The comparison with Jupiter who overthrew his father Cronus to rule the universe would instance Tamburlaine's hubris. Indeed, so strong was the critical belief that Marlowe must conform to this conventional pattern that an argument about his principal characters as 'overreachers' (striving beyond permitted limits and thus being destroyed) became virtually a critical orthodoxy earlier this century. What might be expected is, however, precisely what does not happen in the Tamburlaine plays. There is nothing in the first play and little in the second to challenge Tamburlaine's claims in the above speech and everything to support them. The reference to Jupiter as easily recalls the legend that the god was raised as a shepherd on Mount Ida, confirming Tamburlaine's similarity with Jupiter. The pursuit of power and wealth which Tamburlaine undertakes is marked by success after success. The first *Tamburlaine* play (and the evidence would suggest it was conceived as an independent play, with the second play being devised after its success) ends with Tamburlaine marrying Zenocrate and using the same comparison with the Olympian gods. Tamburlaine celebrates Zenocrate as being like Juno after Jupiter overthrew his father and the other Titans. Rather than mocking Tamburlaine's standing, comparisons with the classical Olympians enhance him. Even the second play's conclusion with Tamburlaine's death reveals him handing on his empire to two of his sons. His advice to them reiterates the philosophy of the speech above: to achieve and to maintain earthly crowns require relentless striving. Although Tamburlaine is clearly not happy about dying, there is nothing to suggest that he is dissatisfied with the outcome of his ambitions.

The plays, therefore, entice us to imagine dramatic worlds ordered differently from those most of Marlowe's contemporaries would have proposed. Tamburlaine's claims, made in poetic language rich in ornament and imagery, are given a dramatic actuality which confronts the everyday. The drama's structure offers a substance to the opulence of Tamburlaine's poetry, confirming his sovereignty of the plays. An audience witnesses this dramatic world on Tamburlaine's terms, a world where his audacious claims are constantly confirmed. Whether Tamburlaine was imagined as a scourge against God or as a scourge unknowingly acting for God, Marlowe offered his audiences the possibility of escape into a world of alternatives, where the proprieties believed to govern society were apparently suspended. The warrior Tamburlaine becomes a painter in poetry and his exaggerated world becomes realized for a few hours. Violence and revolt become aesthetically rich; the end of activity is earthly gratification of wealth and power. It is not that Marlowe tries to force an audience to believe this exaggerated world really exists – or should exist – beyond the theatre; he has given them space and language to imagine differently.

The second example of what I term the Marlowe effect comes from *Doctor Faustus*. Faustus has been momentarily persuaded by an old man to seek repentance and turn to God. Mephostophilis chastises Faustus, who quickly realigns himself with Satan. He asks to see Helen of Troy, whom he has previously conjured, and she returns:

Was this the face that launch'd a thousand ships
And burnt the topless towers of Ilium?
Sweet Helen, make me immortal with a kiss;
Her lips suck forth my soul, see where it flies!
Come Helen, come, give me my soul again;
Here will I dwell, for heaven be in these lips,
And all is dross that is not Helena.
                    Enter Old Man.
I will be Paris, and for love of thee
Instead of Troy shall Wittenberg be sack'd,
And I will combat with weak Menelaus
And wear thy colours on my plumed crest;
Yea, I will wound Achilles in the heel
And then return to Helen for a kiss.
O, thou art fairer than the evening air
Clad in the beauty of a thousand stars;
Brighter art thou than flaming Jupiter
When he appear'd to hapless Semele,
More lovely than the monarch of the sky
In wanton Arethusa's azur'd arms,
And none but thou shalt be my paramour.

Faust. V. i. 97-116

Faustus's evocation of the Trojan War exemplifies Marlowe's interest in characters who desire to take on roles from the past, even when they pose destructive consequences. The apparition of Helen provokes Faustus imaginatively to exaggerate himself into a heroic figure. His imagery stresses the destructive nature of his act – Helen sucks forth his soul; his celebration of her as brighter than Jupiter when he appeared to Semele recalls the myth in which Semele was consumed by fire as a result of sexually enjoying the god in his undisguised form. On one level, this imagery proposes a deluded Faustus who chooses momentary sensual gratification (and this may be only a hellish illusion of Helen, too) instead of Christian eternal joys. Faustus's fantasy even readily allows a crossing of gender – he will be both the male Paris and the female Semele; Helen is both the paragon of female beauty and like the pre-eminently masculine Jupiter. This adoption of shifting gender identity is something which Marlowe excels at playing with (note how it occurs in the passage from *Edward II* in the next example) and often suggests an exotic decadence.

6

Yet, the contrast between the physically decrepit old man and the poetically enhanced beauties of Helen could not be greater. Despite what conventional morality might indicate about this scene, the reader's or audience's sympathies are aesthetically drawn to Faustus's fantasy. Hellish illusion becomes more attractive and desirable than Christian certainties. This is not to propose that Marlowe is here 'of the devil's party'. What he is doing is dramatically forcing the suspension of certain norms which governed an Elizabethan construction of the satanic and Christian, the hellish and heavenly (which in Marlowe's age were understood as realities with firm definitions in ways no longer imagined in Britain). Faustus's creation of a heroic theatre in which he casts himself in a major role is sufficiently alluring for it to linger imaginatively with readers or spectators, regardless whether the play is concluded as a conventional morality or as radically questioning the nature of heaven and hell. The making of the event in poetry undermines attempts to understand it prosaically, and the poetry challenges the assumptions of prosaic understanding.

The third example of the Marlowe effect comes from *Edward II*. At the play's beginning, Edward, having become king, recalls his banished lover Gaveston. The drama opens with Gaveston revelling in his fortune. He imagines how he will maintain his central place with Edward:

> I must have wanton poets, pleasant wits,
> Musicians, that with touching of a string
> May draw the pliant king which way I please:
> Music and poetry is his delight;
> Therefore I'll have Italian masques by night,
> Sweet speeches, comedies and pleasing shows;
> And in the day, when he shall walk abroad,
> Like sylvan nymphs my pages shall be clad;
> My men like satyrs grazing on the lawns,
> Shall with their goat-feet dance an antic hay;
> Sometime a lovely boy in Dian's shape,
> With hair that gilds the water as it glides,
> Crownets of pearl about his naked arms,
> And in his sportful hands an olive-tree,
> To hide those parts which men delight to see,
> Shall bathe him in a spring, and there, hard by,
> One like Actaeon peeping through the grove

Shall by the angry goddess be transformed,
And running in the likeness of an hart,
By yelping hounds pull'd down, and seem to die:
Such things as these best please his majesty.

Ed. II, I. i. 51-71

This scene of opulence and sexual suggestiveness is completely decadent. Queen Elizabeth often used the symbolism of Diana the Huntress to exemplify her own chastity and 'masculine' qualities – thus displaying her fitness as ruler. Here Diana has been transformed into a figure of sexual titillation (and made effeminate by making her a boy!). Actaeon being killed by his own dogs is one of the most disturbing episodes of Ovid's *Metamorphoses*, and it constantly taxed Renaissance ingenuity to allegorize its savagery into some moralized example. Here the episode becomes a voyeuristic amusement where Actaeon merely *seems* to die in a fantasy of sex and death. Gaveston is recreating the Roman emperor Tiberius's sexual adventureland on Capri (used by the historian Suetonius to illustrate the moral corruption of Rome). The scene, therefore, sets up an expectation of Gaveston as a negative influence on Edward. The English nobles' hatred of Gaveston appears to be given foundation, the kingdom seeming to slip into decline through Edward's refusal to give up his pursuit of the sensual. Marlowe appears to be organizing a commonplace dramatic morality, a demonstration that proper self-government is necessary for a monarch.

Such expectations, however, are typically reversed by Marlowe. As the play develops, the nobles' claims to be seeking order in the kingdom is increasingly exposed as their desires to manage the kingdom for their personal advantages. Those claiming to represent the best interests of the state become its greatest rebels and responsible for its disorders. The decadence of Edward and Gaveston appears less and less seriously corrupt as the events unfold. Gaveston may be seeking favours from Edward but his relation with the king combines self-interest with loyalty, whereas the protestations of affection from nobles and Queen Isabella are revealed as deceptive. The play does not suggest there is anything innocent or ideal in Gaveston's and Edward's desires for play, but the contrasting brutality of those ranged against them forces an audience to re-evaluate its response to Gaveston's vision above. Rather than a simple revelation of sensual corruption, Gaveston's excessiveness contrasts with the prosaic, grey but also corrupt world of the English nobles. Marlowe places aesthetic extravagance against philistinism, decadence againt treachery, unsettling his audience because none of the alternatives is ultimately endorsable. They are, though, the alternatives that are proposed, and Gaveston's surfeit of delight comes to seem a more attractive option as the play progresses. Once again, Marlowe uses language and theatre to force spectators to imagine differently, to move outside the conventions theatre had previously used to depict an explicitly secular or sacred morality – the central role of drama before the rise of the commercial theatres. In Marlowe's plays, poetic extravagance and spectacle combine to offer different perspectives to the everyday, offering worlds of new possibilities.

2

Life

The Marlowe effect was a huge success with Renaissance audiences and readers. It helped Marlowe become the most popular playwright (and one of the most popular poets) of the late-Elizabethan and early Jacobean world. From existing records, it would seem that the *Jew of Malta* was the most frequently performed play between 1592 and 1597, with thirty-six recorded performances. *Doctor Faustus* was fourth, with twenty-five performances. In comparison, the most popular Shakespeare play was *Henry VI*, with seventeen performances. Thomas Dekker's plague pamphlet of 1603, *The Wonderful Year*, personified the plague lurking in the suburbs of London as a 'stalking Tamburlaine'. *Tamburlaine* was widely enough known for it to become a source of parody. In 1629 spectators at Bridewell prison were reputed to have greeted the appearance of dungcarts with the second play's 'Holla ye pamper'd jades of Asia!'. Marlowe's erotic epyilla, *Hero and Leander*, was printed in at least nine editions between 1598 and 1637, and his lyric 'The Passionate Shepherd to his Love' was also extremely popular (and has subsequently become one of the most widely known Elizabethan lyrics). As with the plays, Marlowe's poetry was admired by many for its sensual extravagance. Thomas Middleton's *A Mad World, My Masters* (1605/6) describes *Hero and Leander* and Shakespeare's *Venus and Adonis* as 'two luscious marrow-bone pies for a young married wife'. Marlowe's erotic verse found less favour with the Church authorities. His translations of Ovid's *Amores* which were printed without licence were ordered to be burnt in 1599.

Extravagance of word and action was also popularly attributed to the real Christopher Marlowe. Robert Greene accused Marlowe of Machiavellianism and atheism in 1592 (which largely meant Greene felt Marlowe was capable of unprincipled deceit and self-promotion through staging socially heterodox views). Marlowe's violent death from a dagger wound in a Deptford house in 1593 at the age of 29 supported the view of a notorious life. The dramatist Thomas Kyd testified to the authorities that Marlowe owned heretical books. Another acquaintance, Richard Baines, was responsible for crediting Marlowe with the types of opinions a character in Marlowe's plays might advance. Baines claimed in an official deposition that Marlowe 'affirmeth that Moyses was but a jugler & that one Heriots [Thomas Harriot] being Sir W Raleighs man can do more then he'; 'That all they that love not Tobacco & Boies were fooles'; 'That the beginning of Religioun was only to keep men in awe'; that Marlowe had 'as good Right to Coine as the Queene of England'. The contemporary portrait of Marlowe, and the one that has remained in circulation, is of a man living on a dangerous social and intellectual edge. Our knowledge that Marlowe also worked for the Elizabethan secret service has given a new emphasis to his notoriety. Where Shakespeare seems comfortably bourgeois, Marlowe emerges a dangerous romantic figure expounding unorthodox views and involved in espionage and the underworld. Even his name is not fixed. He also appears as Merlin, Morley, Marley, Marlin, and Marlow in contemporary accounts. His contemporary notoriety has led to a modern tradition which sees all the plays' characters as versions of Marlowe the dramatist.

Is there any truth to this romanticized Marlowe, and what is the relation between author and writing? A book on Christopher Marlowe in a series entitled Writers and their Work must use the 'and' which stands between the writer and the work not as an obvious conjunction but to indicate the bringing together of two different centres of critical interest. We know a reasonable amount about Marlowe's life in comparison with most Elizabethan playwrights: we know where he was born, more or less where he lived, something of what he did, and how he died. We also know he was the author of seven plays, a long fragment of an erotic epyilla, translations from Ovid and Lucan, and a few miscellaneous poems; but of the relation of the work to the life we know almost nothing. Unlike nineteenth- or twentieth-century assumptions of a literary writer at the centre of a web of words which have been spun to reveal a controlled structure, the conditions of writing and the understanding of what writing was designed to achieve were very different for a sixteenth-century dramatist. In particular, using literary writing as a means of revealing actual autobiography would have been an alien concept to an Elizabethan. The idea of biography, notably writing the lives of great figures, was important in providing patterns in which to observe virtue and vice, not in capturing individual complexities. Literary writings were not devised to confront authentic experiences in as unmediated a manner as possible. Marlowe's dramatic characters are not designed to appear psychologically realistic in a modern sense, let alone to reflect the personality of the writer.

Marlowe's life and, especially, his death have become the subject of much speculation recently, especially about whether he died as a result of a brawl or was murdered by the secret service. There have equally been efforts to relate the'life to the work and to create various chronologies for the writings. I believe that in an introductory book of this nature it is better to concentrate on what writings we have and to consider what they tell us about the world they circulated in rather than writing at length to confirm or refute often detailed and ingenious theories about the relation of 'the real Christopher Marlowe' to the plays and poems. As the next section will discuss, there is much evidence to suggest that we actually possess little of what Marlowe wrote that has not been subject to later alterations. As a result of his dying young, certainly before the height of his dramatic fame had been reached, his life was open to manipulation by those who wished to have a particular image of Marlowe in circulation. There is no real evidence that he was notorious or heterodox in the ways his posthumous reputation constructed him.

Marlowe was born in 1564 in Canterbury. His father was a shoemaker and he was raised in modest circumstances. The Marlowes were reasonably comfortable, though not prosperous enough to enjoy any settled affluence. Christopher attended a series of small private schools before gaining a scholarship to the King's School, Canterbury, at the age of 14. In 1580 he went up to Cambridge on a scholarship recently established by Archbishop Matthew Parker. Marlowe remained a Parker scholar for six years, receiving his BA in 1584 and his MA in 1587. While at Cambridge, he worked for the Elizabethan secret service. There was some trouble about the granting of his MA, apparently because he was believed to be going to convert to Roman Catholicism and go abroad. In a very unusual step, the Privy Council intervened on his behalf in a resolution dated 29 June 1587

> Whereas it was reported that Christopher Morley was determined to have gone beyond the seas to Reames [Rheims] and there to remain Their

Lordships thought good to certify that he had no such intent, but that in all his accons [actions] he had behaved him selfe, orderlie and discreetelie wherebie he had done Her Majesty good service, and deserved to be rewarded for his faithfull dealinge. . . . It was not her majestie's pleasure that anie one emploied as he had been in matters touching the benefitt of his Countrie should be defamed by those that are ignorant in th'affaires he went about.

According to the terms of the Parker scholarships, Marlowe should have been intending to enter the Church of England. By the time he left Cambridge, however, he seems to have turned to the theatre. The only works we can date with any precision are the two *Tamburlaine* plays and they both seem to have been performed by the end of 1587. After leaving Cambridge, Marlowe seems to have lived mostly in and about London until his death. He appears to have maintained his connection with the secret service. In 1592 he was in Flushing in the Netherlands, where he and Richard Baines were arrested after mutually denouncing each another for counterfeiting money and preparing to defect to the Spanish. Marlowe was sent back to England by the English governor of Flushing, but the charges were not pursued.

Part of the modern fascination with Marlowe's death is that we know more about it and the weeks of his life preceding it than we do about any other period of his life. On 12 May 1593 the dramatist Thomas Kyd with whom Marlowe shared rooms was arrested. This was during one of the frequent periods of unrest among the apprentices of the City of London, and a public libel against foreigners was attributed to Kyd. Kyd's and Marlowe's rooms were searched. Under torture, Kyd claimed papers the authorities described as 'vile and heretical conceits' belonged to Marlowe. Marlowe was not actually taken into custody but, on 20 May, was told to give a daily account of himself to the Privy Council. On 30 May Marlowe died, having spent the day eating and drinking at a house in Deptford with three other figures who had varying degrees of connection with the secret service. The version of events officially accepted at the subsequent inquest was that, in a dispute over the bill, Marlowe had got into a fight with one of the others, who had killed him in self-defence.

Marlowe's sudden death meant he never had an opportunity of answering his defamers and his reputation has become based on uncorroborated and shifty accusations. What we make of the known

13

events of his life depends to a large extent on the inferences we draw from the limited evidence available – inferences largely dependent on our construction of Elizabethan society and its institutions. Far too many biographers of Marlowe explain the events of his life according to reasoning which assumes that society operated along similar patterns to modern ones. The Elizabethan secret service, though, was hardly the precursor of M.I.5 or M.I.6! Generally, there were no government institutions in a modern sense – no standing civil service, police, or other armed forces. The secret service was largely the creation of the zealous Protestant, Sir Francis Walsingham, who ran it (with the help of a government grant) principally to uncover Roman Catholic resistance to Elizabethan policy either in religious practice or through more direct political actions. Most of its agents were no more than paid or coerced informers whose loyalties were various. It is clear that, immediately following his death, there was an organized campaign to present Marlowe as dangerously heterodox and possibly subversive. The English Church, particularly the Archbishop of Canterbury, Whitgift, had a policy of seeking out and punishing those who proclaimed unorthodox viewpoints – mostly extreme Protestant ones – and by this period had no liking for the theatre, so the pressures to discredit Marlowe would have been sympathetically viewed by sections of the Church. There is no hard evidence, though, to link Marlowe's death with the events of the weeks preceding it, and it is easy to enlarge the whole affair into something having far more sinister significance than it is likely to have had. It was a violent age and deaths such as Marlowe's were not uncommon. Marlowe himself had been involved with the authorities in 1589 over his presence at the killing of a William Bradley by Thomas Watson (a poet and classicist). Ben Jonson killed a fellow actor in 1598 in a similar type of brawl. There were never any moves by the authorities to suppress productions of Marlowe's plays, and his reputation as a 'blasphemer' seems to have had a positive effect on his popularity among theatre-goers and readers of his poetry.

What is more important for a study of Marlowe's plays is what we can discern about his life, or the milieu his life was lived in, which can help clarify the agency which promoted the writing. Marlowe was obviously academically gifted and it would appear he or his family saw academic success as a way of gaining social advancement. Although Elizabethan society was, in many respects, more mobile than English society had been previously, there were limited opportunities for social elevation. By gaining an MA from Cambridge, Marlowe became a gentleman, a rank with defined privileges which the word no longer signifies. There is nothing to suggest a religious vocation, but he probably did contemplate the Church as a possible career, as the terms of his Parker scholarship would suggest. The Church was one arena where a gentleman without financial means could be employed (as Donne finally accepted when his secular possibilities were exhausted), though without significant patronage it was unlikely that Marlowe would have had much opportunty to gain a good living. Another possibility was to enter the service of a nobleman, preferably one at court, as a secretary (as Edmund Spenser did). Marlowe chose to pursue, at least temporarily, two less usual occupations, dramatist and spy. Both of these offered employment which might lead to patronage and greater financial security; both involved an interest in acting.

The evidence suggests that Marlowe's work for the secret service was as an *agent provocateur*. One of the authorities' fears was that university students might be persuaded into adopting Roman Catholicism, go abroad, and work to corrupt the state by joining the missions to reclaim England to the Roman Church. From the Privy Council's intervention with the Cambridge authorities on his behalf, it would seem Marlowe acted the part of a student claiming to be swayed to Rome and planning to go to Rheims, where there was a college to train young Englishmen as missionaries. Whether he actually went to Rheims or not, he would have worked to gain the confidences of those genuinely drawn to Rome and then report on them to the authorities. Similarly, in Flushing he was likely to have been employed to pretend he was a counterfeiter so as to entrap those who were genuinely so, though this role may have been used opportunistically. Marlowe's involvement with spying, however, does not automatically support a view of him as an upholder of dangerous or heretical positions. If anything, he may have been drawn into working for Walsingham because of strong Protestant and anti-Catholic convictions. *The Massacre at Paris*, for instance, is a piece of anti-Catholic invective which promotes popular Protestant beliefs about the diabolical nature of the Church of Rome. What Marlowe's activities did do, though, was to draw him into a world where deceptive role-playing allowed differing vantage-points on powerful but opposing systems of beliefs. His secret-service work, however large or small scale it may have been, was certainly not an activity to promote easy adherence to unquestioned certainties.

As a boy in Canterbury, Marlowe would have had the opportunity of watching plays each year, mostly performed by companies of travelling players; at Cambridge there was also a regular diet of university plays. Theatre, though, was undergoing a major transformation during this period. Before the Reformation, the staging of cycles centred on Christian mysteries had been an important activity in cathedral cities such as Canterbury. These plays largely acted as communal displays of received religious morality. With the coming of the Reformation, the cycles were gradually repressed (often with much local opposition), being seen by the English Church as too closely identified with the old Catholic ways. Some of these morality cycles, though, continued to be acted into Marlowe's lifetime. It was not that Protestantism *de facto* opposed theatre. Initially, the Reformers had seen the theatre as a powerful instrument to aid their own religious ends and had performed Protestant moralities. In Marlowe's time there remained vestiges of a tradition of Protestant dramaturgy in the classically derived humanist Latin dramas performed in the universities (alongside ribald university comedies). By the 1580s, though, a new Protestant establishment had generally become wary of plays, seeing them, along with other forms of illicit pleasure such as brothels and gaming-houses, as places of disorder and irreligion. Puritan elements in the City of London sponsored the former actor and playwright Stephen Gosson (who was born in the same parish as Marlowe) to write a condemnation of playhouses in the *Schoole of Abuse* in 1579. One of Gosson's principal complaints against the stage was that it tempted people to abandon their proper callings with vain dreams of instant wealth and rank.

Such attacks upon the stage testify to a new type of theatre which was rapidly developing when Marlowe decided to participate in it – the commercial theatres based around recognized, and, to some extent, protected, companies of actors performing in purpose-built playhouses in the Liberties of London. The Liberties were the areas just outside London's city walls which were free of the City's regulatory controls and yet, paradoxically, belonged to the City. As Steven Mullaney claims in *The Place of the Stage*, the Liberties 'were places of a complex and contradictory sort of freedom, ambivalent zones of transition between one realm of authority and another'. Locating the playhouses in the Liberties gave the theatre a type of cultural licence. It could enact and represent aspects of Elizabethan culture which were not permitted to be displayed within the City's walls. Audiences could resort to them, as to the brothels, taverns, and bear-baiting pits, to partake of something different from the everyday, the expectation of entertainment which offered escape from the ordinary.

This is not to imply that the theatres were free to stage anything they pleased. The companies of players had to be licensed and, by 1590, the manuscript of each new play performed had to be approved by the Master of the Revels. But this form of state censorship also needs to be seen from contemporary Elizabethan rather than modern perspectives. There were no clear norms on what was prohibited and what permitted, no consistent political, moral, or cultural criteria used by the censors. The precise historical circumstances seem to have determined the Master of the Revel's response to each play, conforming in some respects with the office's original courtly role in ensuring decorum in court entertainments. The censor's role seems to have been to prevent the theatres disrupting public order rather than insisting upon ideological orthodoxy. In the surviving manuscript of the multi-authored *Sir Thomas More* (1594), for example, there are instances where the censor intervened to change specific features but nothing to indicate that there were fundamental objections to the play's favourable presentation of the Roman Catholic More who had been executed by Henry VIII.

Given his popularity, Marlowe's imaginative extravagances were obviously exactly the displays which audiences sought in the playhouses of the Liberties. His plays' presentation of figures from apparently humble origins who rise to fame and notoriety (e.g. Tamburlaine, Faustus, Gaveston, Spencer) are far more likely to reflect the collective desires of a popular audience for imaginative escape from the closely defined social structures they experienced in the City than to indicate Christopher Marlowe's aspirations to go beyond permitted norms in real life. The popular success of Marlowe's plays probably rested on their offering audiences of this new commercial theatre something of the vain dreams of wealth and rank zealous Protestant critics decried the stage for offering. Marlowe participated in a theatre which had divorced itself from seeking to represent communal religious moralities. Locating the playhouses in the Liberties exemplifies how the theatre had become an institution perceived as offering something which necessarily occupied a space outside the boundaries of the commune. Where medieval moralities had been staged before churches, plays now addressed audiences that had momentarily left the bounds of convention and were looking for some type of release from the institutions which normally contained the community. Where audiences had previously participated in the triumph of Christian morality, they now chose to witness the Jew of Malta, Barabas, the unprincipled deceiver whose actions reek havoc among an entire population in a play which reveals a universal hypocrisy. Marlowe could choose as his principal figures: a Jew whose namesake is the thief freed instead of Christ, a Doctor of learning who sells his soul to Satan, an exotic non-European tyrant known for his cruelty, an English king who has a homosexual lover and who is overthrown by a treacherous subject and an adulterous queen. These were now the types of displays audiences wished to see enacted. Marlowe recognized the financial possibilities in writing popular plays and, had he lived, it is likely he could have made some sort of living as a professional dramatist. As the payment of £4 in 1602 by the theatre company The Admiral's Men to William Bride and Samuel Rowley for additions to *Doctor Faustus* illustrates, there was money in Marlowe.

In the new commercial theatre Marlowe found a medium to voice his sceptical and ironic view of humanity's varying conditions. This intellectual perspective is likely to have developed during his university years, being nurtured through his readings in the Classics. Classical literature was the staple of the university curriculum, where all students took a general arts degree (at both BA and MA levels). Latin was the medium of the university, and a student was encouraged to become acquainted with a wide body of classical texts to provide examples and precepts for the displays of oratory and rhetoric on which success in study was assessed. Marlowe's translations of Ovid's *Amores* and of the first book of Lucan's epic of Roman civil war, *The Pharsalia*, suggest he was attracted to classical texts which deal with deception, civil disorder, and ungovernable emotions both in private and civic life. Although there is nothing which indicates these translations were produced during Marlowe's Cambridge years, it is likely that he examined both Ovid and Lucan in some detail there (certainly Ovid, though not the *Amores*, was a seminal author of both Elizabethan grammar school and university). We do not know when Marlowe's *All Ovids Elegies* was first published, as it was unlicensed and claims on its title-page to be

18

printed at Middlebourgh (in the Netherlands); it probably first appeared in the 1590s. *Lucan's First Book* was entered for publication in 1593 but did not actually appear until 1600.

At both the King's School in Canterbury and later at Cambridge, Marlowe would have been introduced to Renaissance Humanism. Humanism's belief in the Latin and Greek Classics as models of eloquence and virtue and its promotion of literary writings as important in developing the skills needed for public life (which a university education was designed to provide for young men) promoted the availability of a good range of texts and stimulated an enthusiasm to read widely in classical literature. As important for Marlowe was the fact that humanistic practices promoted the development of the subjective reader. The practice of imitation which underlay the study of the Classics in schools and university rested in innovation through classical literature not merely repeating the originals. This demonstrated the speaker's or writer's knowledge of the original's principles but it also promoted using the Classics as a means of negotiating all types of knowledge, encouraging different and distinctive thought and expression. As recent criticism has shown, these subjective possibilities did not lead to an unfettered sense of individualism. Rather, humanistic practices encouraged taking on different guises to speak in a variety of ways, a protean self-fashioning through which to explore the validity of the existing orders of accepted truths.

The logic of Humanism accepted that discourse might be organized to be compelling without being formally valid. This encouraged a belief that eloquent language might reach beyond the bounds of normal reality, ideally to demonstrate the divinity above human reason – the principal argument for the importance of poetry in Sir Philip Sidney's *Defence of Poetry*, for example. However, it also encouraged a belief in scepticism, recognizing that the world could be alluringly constructed in a language which collided with assumed truth either because the eloquence was deceptive or because the eloquence revealed assumed truths as suspect. The dispute – the formal debate where a premiss was defended or opposed according to which roles the participants were assigned – was the forum where the reading practices and oratorical skills developed by humanistic educational practices were most importantly displayed in the system within which Marlowe was educated. Although sixteenth-century schools and universities were hardly arenas of intellectual freedom,

Marlowe's education would have done more to facilitate than oppose his opportunities to think against the grain of received opinion, to question the assumed and to assert the unusual.

Christopher Marlowe was hardly a 'typical Elizabethan', but there is no evidence to confirm the romanticized and intellectually dangerous character his reputation has tended to make him. In the end we know virtually nothing about Marlowe as a writer or thinker except through the works which bear his name. It is not even clear, however, that these plays and poems should be seen as the unique product of Christopher Marlowe, 1564–93.

3

Texts

In 1612 Sir Thomas Bodley, founder of the Bodleian Library in Oxford, wrote to his first librarian, Thomas James: 'I can see no good reason to alter my opinion for excluding books as almanacs, plays, and infinite number, that are daily printed, of very unworthy matters.' The inclusion of 'baggage books' among serious texts, Bodley believed, would devalue the library and cause 'scandal'. Bodley was stating no more than the widespread contemporary view that English plays, printed in cheap popular octavo or quarto editions, were not serious literature but popular writings of no particular status. It was only in 1616, when Ben Jonson included some plays in the folio volume (an expensive format to print in) of his *Workes*, that readers were asked to accept English plays as worth their attention as serious literature. The success of Jonson's volume prompted Heminge and Condell to edit a folio of Shakespeare's plays in 1623: *Mr William Shakespeares Comedies Histories & Tragedies. Published according to the True Originall Copies.*

There was never a folio of Marlowe's plays and poems. Where Jonson saw his own work through the press or Shakespeare's first editors were keen to emphasize that they were printing plays from original copies, Marlowe's plays were printed haphazardly in the cheap octavo and quarto editions Sir Thomas Bodley insisted should not be found in a serious collection. This has important implications for our understanding of the relation of author to text and what we are actually reading when we sit down with a modern edition of Christopher Marlowe's works.

The only Marlowe texts to be published during his lifetime were the two plays of *Tamburlaine* which first appeared in 1590. Unless readers already knew who the author was, however, they would have had no clue to who wrote the plays, as Marlowe's name is not to be found on the title-page nor anywhere in the edition (the first text of *Tamburlaine* to carry Marlowe's name is 1820!). Further, the printer Richard Jones informs his readers in the preface that he has purposely left out some 'fond and frivolous gestures' (low comic scenes) because he does not consider them appropriate to 'so honourable and stately a history'. Jones admits, though, that these scenes were enjoyed by the audiences when the plays were performed. In other words, even in an edition printed during the writer's lifetime, there is a complete absence of any authority that we are reading the *Tamburlaine* plays as Marlowe wrote them and evidence to indicate we are not. What would *Tamburlaine* have been like with comic scenes? Perhaps it would have been more like the 1616 edition of *Doctor Faustus*, where comic figures (often labelled 'clowne' meaning simpletons) parody the serious conjuring of Faustus. Certainly, watching a Tamburlaine whose unbroken progression of bloody victories and poetic exclamations were interrupted by 'fond and frivolous gestures' would provoke a very different context for our experience of Tamburlaine's management of theatre.

Although Elizabethan plays were frequently written by one individual and ascribed to him (for example, the 1594 quarto of *Edward II* clearly announces it was 'Written by Chri. Marlow Gent.'), collaboration among a variety of writers was also frequent. The earliest edition of *Dido, Queen of Carthage* (1594) tells us the play was written by Christopher Marlowe and Thomas Nashe, who alludes admiringly to Marlowe in *The Unfortunate Traveller*. It is not possible, however, to discern the Marlowe sections from the Nashe sections of *Dido*. Indeed, it is not clear whether they collaborated closely or whether Nashe was simply responsible for preparing a text for printing after Marlowe's death. Marlowe's name is given prominence on the title-page, but this may simply reflect the printer's belief that Marlowe's name would be better for sales than Nashe's. Elizabethan playwrights did not prepare their texts for publication. Plays were sold to an acting company whose interest was in producing something an audience wished to pay to see. If it was felt a play should be altered to give it a greater chance of being successfully staged, particularly in a later revival, the companies had no hesitation in making changes. As we saw in the last section, two playwrights were paid £4 for additions to *Doctor Faustus* in 1602 (the earliest text we have of *Faustus* is 1604).

In contrast to English drama, poetry was seen as serious literature, but the printing of poetry in the sixteenth century also rarely involved the author. A poet such as Edmund Spenser believed that serious poetic works, such as his *Faerie Queene*, should be presented in a well-prepared format, but a great deal of shorter lyric poetry was circulated in manuscripts among friends and associates. Virtually none of Donne's poetry was published during his lifetime, for instance; yet Donne's verse was well known through manuscript circulation. Marlowe's poetry also shows no evidence of his preparing it for the press. *Hero and Leander*, Marlowe's most substantial poetic work, is an unfinished fragment that was eventually 'completed' by George Chapman. Chapman's continuation of the poem (which is as long as Marlowe's sections) was clearly distinguished from Marlowe's when the poems were first published in 1598, but Chapman's additions transform the nature of *Hero and Leander*, bringing attention to moral proprieties ignored in Marlowe's sections.

The short lyric poem 'The Passionate Shepherd to his Love' is a telling example of the problem of attribution and composition of Marlowe's texts. This was an extremely popular poem in Renaissance England and exists in four noticeably different versions. Most modern editors choose to follow the one printed in the collection known as *England's Helicon* in 1600, where the poem is attributed to Marlowe. The poem was first published, though, in 1599 in a shorter four-stanza version in a collection called *The Passionate Pilgrim*, and this version was widely circulated in manuscript collections, where it is often attributed to Sir Philip Sidney or Sir Walter Ralegh. In the mid-seventeenth century, Izaak Walton knew the lyric as Marlowe's poem but printed it in his 1655 *Complete Angler* with an additional stanza which also appears in early manuscript collections but which virtually all modern editions ignore. There are only reasonable grounds for accepting the poem as Marlowe's (as discussed below, it is parodied in *The Jew of Malta*), but there is no absolute certainty about authorship and considerable grounds for speculation about what 'Marlowe's' poem may originally have looked like. This one brief lyric indicates problems which are only intensified with the longer texts!

Most modern readers using student editions of Marlowe's plays normally assume that they are reading the words of Christopher Marlowe as he wrote them, or that a modern editor, having carefully weighed the evidence, has selected a reading which is substantially what the writer intended. In Marlowe's case such assumptions are unquestionably desires for imaginary authentic texts on the part of editors and their readers. The location of the real Marlowe texts, as with the search for the real Christopher Marlowe, is an impossibility. Editors wish to restore the unamended words of the author, but Elizabethan drama is not amenable to this pursuit. Editorial interpretation will always promote as authentic a constructed version of a work which conforms with an editorial policy conditioned by the editor's own intentions.

This is not to propose that we have nothing of what Marlowe wrote. Although Marlowe's name does not appear on the first edition of *Tamburlaine*, there is no doubt he was responsible for originating the performed plays and that most of the printed text is probably close to what he wrote. Marlowe clearly had a great deal to do with all the works which bear his name, but even relatively small changes can substantially alter our understanding of a text's design and meaning. Rather than being only a specialized interest of editors, questions about Marlowe's texts confront every serious reader. The problems involved with Marlowe's texts and the implications for our understanding of their meanings can be illustrated through two examples.

The earliest edition we possess of Marlowe's most popular play, *The Jew of Malta*, is 1633, forty years after Marlowe died. Numerous commentators have noted the difference in the quality of the writing between the first two acts and the last three, though there is no collaborating evidence to suggest another writer was involved. In Act IV Barabas's Turkish slave, Ithamore, has fallen in love with a courtesan who is using him in order to blackmail Barabas. The courtesan, Bellamira, proposes that she will marry Ithamore. He replies in a speech of Marlovian eloquence:

> Content, but we will leave this paltry land,
> And sail from hence to Greece, to lovely Greece:
> I'll be thy Jason, thou my golden fleece;
> Where painted carpets o'er the meads are hurl'd,
> And Bacchus' vineyards overspread the world,
> Where woods and forests go in goodly green;
> I'll be Adonis, thou shalt be Love's Queen;
> The meads, the orchards, and the primrose-lanes,
> Instead of sedge and reed, bear sugar-canes:
> Thou in those groves, by Dis above,
> Shalt live with me and be my love.

Jew, IV. ii. 106-16

This speech is uncharacteristic of Ithamore in the play. Like many of Marlowe's characters, Ithamore lets us know that his birth is 'mean' and his profession 'what you please' (*Jew*, II. ii. 170-1). As he informs us, his activities to date have not included being a poet. He has spent his time:

> In setting Christian villages on fire,
> Chaining of eunuchs, binding galley-slaves.
> One time I was an hostler in an inn,
> And in the night time secretly would I steal
> To travellers' chambers, and there cut their throats.
> Once at Jerusalem, where the pilgrims kneel'd,
> I strewed powder on the marble stones,
> And therewithal their knees would rankle so,
> That I have laugh'd a-good to see the cripples
> Go limping home to Christendom on stilts.

Jew, II. iii. 208-17

Ithamore's speech to his courtesan recalls Faustus's creation of a heroic theatre for himself and Helen. The speech, in one light, looks like an example of the Marlowe effect, where there is a display of eloquence which helps to challenge conventional orders for understanding. The slave, Ithamore, seems to be given the capacity for heroic passion shared by Marlovian characters such as Tamburlaine or Faustus.

In fact, the speech is a comic parody of Tamburlaine's or Faustus's eloquence. Besides comments which make it clear Ithamore is ugly and in rags (emphasizing the duplicity of the whore who only wants the Jew's money and Ithamore's abandoned sense of reality in his passion's fantasy), Ithamore's speech itself does not attain the lyrical integrity he is striving to imitate. The lines are consciously parodying Marlowe's most famous lyric, 'The Passionate Shepherd to his Love' and indicating Ithamore's inability to use this language properly. The reference to 'Dis above', for example, is completely misguided, as Dis is the god of the underworld!

Ithamore's speech adds to the general demonstration of hypocrisy that underlies *The Jew of Malta*, where each scene reveals corruption and deception in a universal desire for gold and power. But in another respect it is quite crude and consciously structured to mock the inflated rhetoric frequently employed by Marlowe's characters.

Is it Marlowe playfully parodying himself or is this a later parody of Marlowe which has been added?

When *The Jew of Malta* was revived in 1633 for performance at court by the Queen's Company, Thomas Heywood wrote a preface for it in which he stresses that it is an old play and somewhat unfashionable. The preface certainly does not suggest that *The Jew of Malta* was perceived as a serious piece; its revival appears to have taken place because of the notoriety of its principal character, Barabas. This unfashionable quality might indicate that the text was felt to require comic aspects which parodied Marlovian extravagance as a means of playfully mocking the play's old-fashioned quaintness. Further evidence that Marlowe's reputation in the seventeenth century was not based on witnessing his plays as exhibitions of serious drama is also offered by Edmund Gayton, who disapprovingly recalls popular Caroline audiences in his *Pleasant Notes upon Don Quixot* (1654). What is interesting is that, while Gayton reveals some continuing popularity for Marlowe's plays (they are still insisted upon by the audience, despite the actors wanting to perform something else), performances of them have become increasingly reductive, staging only those parts the audience wants to see and not the plays as wholes:

> I have known upon one of these Festivals, but especially at Shrove-tide, where the players have been appointed, notwithstanding their bils to the contrary, to act what a major part of the company [the audience] had a mind to; sometimes *Tamerlane*, sometimes *Jurgurtha* [a play not by Marlowe], sometimes *The Jew of Malta*, and sometimes parts of all these, and at last, none of the three taking, they were forc'd to undresse and put off their tragick habits, and conclude the day with *The Merry Milkmaides*.

Given this environment, it is not difficult to imagine an acting company in the 1630s, when the text for *The Jew of Malta* originates, wishing to include as many possible displays of 'the Marlowe effect' as it could, even, or perhaps especially, a mocking of it. The 1663 quarto of *Doctor Faustus* adds a scene plagiarized from *The Jew of Malta* which testifies to this type of continuing interest in *The Jew*, though by this point such additions are really a long way from possible origins with Marlowe. On the other hand, in defence of Ithamore's speech as a thoroughly Marlovian creation, we are told by the printer of *Tamburlaine* that there were comic scenes performed in these two plays and not printed, and *Doctor Faustus* has some parodic comic scenes (though the question of authorial attribution in these is also problematic). We cannot determine with any accuracy whether Ithamore's speech is genuinely by Marlowe, an adaptation, or some later addition to heighten a Marlowe effect among audiences who wished to see parodies of Marlovian eloquence. The 1633 edition of *The Jew of Malta* is the only early version of the play we possess and we can only accept its text as more-or-less Marlowe's authentic one.

A similar but much more crucial variant of the problem of 'what is Marlowe?' and what merely Marlowesque is provided by *Doctor Faustus*. *Faustus* is unique among Marlowe's plays because we possess two substantial versions of it. Actually we have two different plays: an A version first printed in 1604 and a B version which is half as long again as A printed in 1616. It is not that the A version is incomplete; in fact, most modern critics prefer it aesthetically and there have been important recent editions of its text. The B version (which is the basis of the text printed in most student editions) is extended largely by comic material which parodies the serious action of the play. It also includes some different serious scenes, too, and in general forces the play to conform much more to a traditional morality pattern than the A version does.

At the play's conclusion, for example, the A version finishes with Faustus being led off by Mephostophilis. It is not clear what the nature of Faustus's damnation will be, and, as we move to the final chorus's suggestion that, in regarding Faustus's 'hellish fall', the wise will realize 'Only to wonder at unlawful things', strongly sceptical possibilities are being offered about the precise nature of heaven and hell. Jonathan Dollimore's important argument in *Radical Tragedy* about the transgressive nature of Faustus's deliberate rejection of the heavenly is given interesting emphasis by the A version of the play, which refuses a conventional portrayal of heaven or hell, helping to prompt greater questioning about the actual nature of both. By contrast, the B version's depiction of Faustus's transgression is of an act which catapults him into the hand of tormenting devils, re-inforcing a more conventional morality pattern and reducing our opportunities to read the final chorus ironically. In the B version, after Faustus's departure with Mephostophilis, a scene is added in which scholars discover Faustus's ripped-up limbs the following morning:

The devils whom Faustus served have torn him thus:
For twixt the hours of twelve and one, methought
I heard him shriek and call aloud for help,
At which self time the house seemed all on fire
With dreadful horror of these damned fiends.

Faust. V. iii. 8-12

It could be construed, then, that the B version of *Doctor Faustus* is an expansion of Marlowe's play to make it conform with the morality pattern it was felt a Jacobean audience would be comfortable with and to introduce more high jinks in the comic scenes to satisfy the audience's desire for farce: comedies, far more than tragedies, were the staple of the Elizabethan and Jacobean theatre. Money was paid to revise *Faustus* in 1602 and there was a popular comic genre concerned with magicians.

In other respects, however, the B version of *Faustus* is equally as transgressive as A but in a different fashion. Both versions have a scene where a horse trader is tricked into believing he has pulled off Faustus's leg. The scene is much expanded upon in the B version, which also has another trickery scene where Faustus's head is apparently cut off. It could be argued that Faustus's final dismemberment is a serious culmination to these sequences of faked theatrical dismemberment. Equally, the actor playing Faustus will shortly appear (one trusts restored!) before the audience after the concluding chorus to receive the acknowledgement for his performance, qualifying this last dismemberment and acknowledging that, in one sense, it is no more real than the previous ones. This mixing of trickery and actuality deliberately obscures their limits and prevents a clear definition of the play's comic or tragic potentials.

The B version, therefore, heightens the importance of theatricality which is present in both versions, deliberately confusing the limits between 'reality' and 'playing' in *Doctor Faustus*. Since a performance of *Faustus* in the theatre parodies the serious business of saving or damning souls which is the province of religion, the B version can be seen as a much more effective instrument in dissolving the boundaries between comic and tragic. The whole play becomes a piece of spectacle where the limits between comic parody and tragic reality, the farcical and the serious, become impossible to determine with any ease. The B version powerfully transgresses the serious 'theatres' of heaven and hell. Far more than the A text, it is an example of what Mikhail Bakhtin's *Rebelais and his World* identifies as the carnivalesque quality of Renaissance culture, where powerful abstract concerns, such as heaven and hell, were reduced to some form of grotesque material representation, allowing them to be laughed at (think of the display of the seven deadly sins in *Faustus*). As Bakhtin argues, the use of carnival de-centres fixed orders, allowing other possibilities and revealing the relativity of established authorities' claims to know the world's structure. From this perspective, the B version of Faustus becomes a powerful challenge to the orders of established religion through its mockery of its norms and confusion over Faustus's theatrical foolery (pretending to have his limbs severed) and his apparent actual dismemberment by the devils. Religion, as much as theatre, could be imagined as a bag of tricks.

My point in this analysis (these ideas in *Faustus* will be further explored below) is to illustrate how questions of which text might more accurately be claimed to resemble Marlowe's authentic one are intricately caught up with the critical structures for interpretation we bring to the texts. Michel Foucault's 'What is an Author' considers our construction of 'the author-function':

> aspects of an individual which we designate as making him an author are only a projection . . . of the operations that we force texts to undergo, the connections that we make, the traits that we establish as pertinent, the continuities that we recognise, or the exclusions that we practice.

It is likely that neither the A nor the B version of *Doctor Faustus* represents the play that was performed throughout the 1590s or the one Christopher Marlowe wrote sometime between the late 1580s and his death. The two versions, though, are the most telling example of the difficulties we face if we come to Marlowe imagining we can determine a chronology to his writings or that the texts we possess are precisely as the author wrote them. Rather than the collected dramatic works of one author, what 'Marlowe' represents is the evolution into texts of a number of powerful theatrical depictions which originated with Christopher Marlowe but which were subsequently negotiated and transformed within English Renaissance culture. For some readers, this loss of Marlowe as an individual consciousness revealing closely determined intentions in his texts may be a more challenging feature than confronting some of the unsettling ideas the plays and poetry contain. Our culture has come to think of Marlowe as one of the 'golden-age' writers, occupying an important pedestal in an Elizabethan hall of fame. Yet, in Marlowe's own time, a play's possibilities of spurring any type of lasting interest were precarious (the second most popular play of the 1590s has not survived at all!). Recall Gayton's description of the players who, having tried to please the crowd with *Tamburlaine* and *The Jew of Malta*, were finally forced to abandon their 'tragick habits' and act '*The Merry Milkmaides*'. Marlowe's texts reflect the material conditions of this culture far more than we usually allow for. More than any other English Renaissance writer, Marlowe exemplifies how the conditions of early modern literature were fundamentally different from the norms which govern later centuries. Perhaps we should read or imagine these texts differently from the ways we have been used to, concentrating more on what they tell us about the relations between drama and the culture it participated in than imagining these play-texts as the controlled vision of the individual author.

4

Dramatic Proposals

In a public letter addressed to Sir Walter Ralegh which prefaced his *Faerie Queene*, Edmund Spenser claims the purpose of his poem is 'to fashion a gentleman or noble person in vertuous or gentle discipline'. Sir Philip Sidney's *Defence of Poetry* argued that mankind, as a creature sharing in God's image, is best displayed in poetry: 'when with the force of a divine breath, he bringeth things forth far surpassing her [nature's] doing.' Sidney argues that through poetic creation humanity gains an intimation of the unfallen perfect world lost with the sin of Adam. Spenser's and Sidney's assertions are illustrations of the morally elevating claims made for the power of literature in the Renaissance world.

Marlowe's drama is a sustained assault on preconceptions about a didactic role for literature, imagining it to improve the human condition through representing reductive attitudes about moral improvement. Marlowe's scepticism about this role for writing, and of the values which underlie it, reflects the cultural diversities of sixteenth-century life. As we have seen above, his intellectual training and the possibilities offered by the new commercial theatre available in London combined to provide him with opportunities to challenge received conventions and norms. Earlier this century, critical attempts were made to present Elizabethan society and culture as ordered and stable, a benignly hegemonic world where the country unquestioningly adhered to the accepted ideology of the establishment. Much recent research by both historians and literary critics has displayed this Elizabethan world-picture as a modern-day myth and we are now aware of a cultural complexity which defies easy definition.

Marlowe's writing reflects the turbulence of the Elizabethan world, but we should not regard its challenge of convention as an attempt to supply new norms. Marlowe is neither a satirist nor a moralist with an organized agenda of opposition and reform; nor do his texts seek to express a developed alternative philosophy. He appears a writer of plentitude, aiming at generating new possibilities, but there is something fragmentary about what he creates. Perhaps it is this lack of resolution in ideas and even in the literary structures he employs which has led to frequent critical uncertainty about his drama, an uncertainty which can sometimes verge on disappointment.

Stephen Greenblatt's *Marvellous Possessions* has recently explored the rhetoric of wonder in Renaissance travel-writing and there is a useful analogy with Marlowe's drama, partly because his plays extensively employ an exotic quality in the foreign as a vehicle to generate spectacle. In general, the plays' excitement rests with their capacity to startle and create the marvellous or unexpected through their extravagance of language and action. Greenblatt notes how the rhetoric of wonder found in travel-writing emerges from encounters with the unexpected and the intense curiosity that arises through this 'excitement of discontinuous wonders'. This recognition that the aesthetic compulsion of wonder stems from discontinuity (and that what helps create its excitement is that it does not comply with expected schemes and remains, in some sense, unaccountable and fragmentary) helps explain Marlovian drama's continuing ability to excite interest despite critical frustrations about accounting for its inconsistencies. Where a critical key to unlock 'Marlowe' has been put forward (such as the unifying concept of 'the overreacher' – characters who are compelled to stretch beyond permitted means and ostensibly suffer for it), the plays have, effectively, had to be critically rewritten to accommodate them to the desired pattern. Rather, Marlowe's success rests precisely in his refusal to adopt an overarching scheme, to generate instead the unexpected and the unaccountable. His plays draw attention to the features in human existence which create instability, which unsettle cultural security but which compel attraction through their sense of the exotic, the forbidden.

As Gaveston's elaborate descriptions of the shows he will perform for Edward which we examined above remind us, exotic differences do not have to occur only in distant places; they can be imported. Marlowe's drama illustrates how the theatre in Elizabethan England had become one of the sites where the exotic could be performed, a parallel to the market-place where unusual foreign goods are displayed in order to be bought and accommodated within the normality of the surrounding world. This parallel with the market is important when we remember that it was a commercial theatre which Marlowe largely wrote for, a place where audiences had to be enticed to subscribe to the dramatic illusions being offered. This theatre looked to displays of the unusual as one of its principal means to generate interest in itself. In Shakespeare's *The Tempest* a feature which the clowns Stephano and Trinculo share with the greedy nobles Sebastian and Antonio is their instant recognition that Caliban is a marketable commodity because unusual in appearance: 'When they will not give a doit to relieve a lame beggar, they will lay out ten to see a dead Indian,' exclaims Trinculo. An audience would also, of course, pay to see Caliban, a fictional creation in a drama which recreated the foreign on the imaginary terms audiences could assimilate. As with Gaveston's desires to captivate Edward – both to amuse him with wonders and in so doing to make him a captive to Gaveston's desires – Marlowe's drama offered audiences brief opportunities to witness the exotic, seeking to capture their money in the admission price they would pay to see this spectacle.

Homi Bhabha has proposed that the impact of the foreign on a culture activates mechanisms within the culture to assimilate it. Bhabha in 'The Commitment to Theory' argues this never entirely happens; rather the foreign is drawn into the 'inbetween', a zone of intersection in which all culturally determined significations are called into question by the unresolved hybridities which are generated. Although Marlowe's writing is clearly not foreign to the culture which produced it, this model seems to me a profitable one in considering his drama. It is as though the exotic foreign and the culturally familiar occur simultaneously in Marlovian drama. *Doctor Faustus* has a structure derived from a conventional morality play in which the transgressor of God's commands falls into damnation; yet, the play also presents Faustus as anything but a typical sinful transgressor warranting his ultimate fate. He is an exotic traveller whose escapades provoke both merriment and wonder. While the play's overall structure acts to try to assimilate Faustus to a morality tradition, the episodic experiences we witness resist such an easy condemnation of his actions. The play creates its own foreign and familiar, it demonstrates mechanisms to absorb the foreign and those to resist it and this is typical of Marlowe's drama. The result is a seemingly unresolvable cultural hybridity, a dispute between accommodating the strange to the familiar and a destabilization of the familiar through its inability to absorb the unexpected. The very qualities which confirm Tamburlaine's barbarian tyranny, such as the massacre of the virgins before Damascus, become the aspects which compel our wonder at his spectacle of power. Marlowe readily recognized that the moment of satisfying theatre is not necessarily a moment of satisfying moral didacticism.

5

Imitation

Marlowe's critique of convention was not unique within Renaissance culture and shared the same roots of intellectual scepticism manifested by a writer such as Montaigne. For Marlowe, a powerful model was the writing of Ovid, the author who challenged the officially sanctioned culture of Augustan Rome. Ovid's urbanity, his sense of black humour, his blending of pathos and farce are qualities equally manifested by Marlowe's writing. He found in the Roman author a host of examples of how to counter a literary establishment which wanted to celebrate human life as potentially open to the control of a narrowly defined moral reason but which denied the attractions of the irrational and uncontrollable side of human affairs.

In Marlowe's time, Ovid had long been used in schools as an example of Latin eloquence. Drawing on medieval conventions which believed that pagan classical literature could only be demonstrated as acceptable in Christian society if it could be shown to promote virtue, a dominant pedagogic tradition of the moralized Ovid existed in Elizabethan England. What Ovid wrote about, and particularly the stories of the *Metamorphoses*, were transformed through allegorical readings which attempted to neutralize their overt sexuality and admission of irrationality among both gods and humanity. Ovid was seldom read in the Renaissance without an accompanying commentary explaining what 'he really meant', forcing his texts to acknowledge accepted Christian virtues – a wonderful example of the foreign being assimilated to the norms of the dominant culture. A strong Renaissance humanist conviction was that eloquence in language demonstrated well-governed and virtuous qualities of mind. Ovid was an elegant stylist and, as a result of the scholarly tradition which insisted on accompanying allegorical glosses to explain his texts' supposed meanings, his writing during Marlowe's time could also be shown to demonstrate approved Christian principles.

Another side of the humanist tradition, however (one which

gained impetus through Reformation beliefs in the importance of the individual encounter with the Bible without mediation by Church authority), was to promote a reading of the Classics without the substantial additions supplied by later commentators. The qualities of the original text itself were stressed, and this led readers to see that, far from being a moralist, Ovid celebrated human sexuality in an uncompromisingly physical way, proposing that sex was something humanity could not control. Further, Ovid detailed a supernatural government of human affairs in which the gods and goddesses were themselves victims of unreasonable passions. Rather than being models of conduct, the gods were more dangerous than irrational mortals because they were more powerful. Ovid's vision of the world is one governed by sudden mutation, not measured justice; like Marlowe, nothing is ever quite what it seems. For the Renaissance reader who saw the Classics as models for eloquence, Ovid was a distinct challenge to the idea that stylistic propriety in literature indicated moral propriety. Instead of providing intimations of the pre-lapsarian world of Adam, Ovidian writing revelled in the shifting and corrupting nature of human passion.

Marlowe's translation of Ovid's *Amores* which appeared as *All Ovid's Elegies* demonstrates his determination to emphasize Ovid's refusal of conventional morality. The collection records the sexual mischief engaged in by the poetic narrator, his mistress Corrina (who is married), and various other women. In Elizabethan England, where the Petrarchan convention of celebrating one's mistress as a model of chaste virtue was fashionable among many English poets, Marlowe's translation succeeded in capturing Ovid's morally un-troubled record of sexual antics. For example, *Elegy*, III. vi, is a lengthy account of the narrator's inability to gain an erection when attempting to have sex with an unnamed woman. She is skilled in sexual arousal and role-playing ('Pure rose she, like a nun to sacrifice, | Or one that with her tender brother lies'), but nothing seems to work. Finally, in disgust she turns him out of bed and has to pour water on the place 'lest her maid should know of her disgrace'. Only in recalling the events does the narrator suddenly find himself with an erection. In 1599, when the Church authorities became aware of Marlowe's work circulating in unapproved editions, they ordered all copies burnt, the only instance of his writing being officially condemned.

Importantly, Marlowe's translation of the *Amores* was an

opportunity to articulate the idea that deception is a usual, and in some cases desired, feature of human existence. 'Admir'd I am of those that hate me most,' claims Machevill [Machiavelli] at the opening of *The Jew of Malta*. 'Though some speak openly against my books, | Yet will they read me, and thereby attain to Peter's chair.' In addition to managed deceptions for the pursuit of power, Marlowe's drama displays a desired self-deception which Ovid's poems characterize, a deliberate refusal to accept the truth and prefer the image. Faustus claims that heaven is in the lips of Helen, even though he has used diabolical forces to conjure her and she may be no more than an illusion. Ovid's exploration of a human capacity for deceiving others as well as self-deception was important for Marlowe, providing examples of such dilemmas examined with comic sympathy and without easy moral condemnation. Ovid, like Marlowe, is no moral satirist. Human failings are exposed not to chastise them as avoidable excesses but because they are apparently an intrinsic part of our condition:

> Seeing thou art fair, I bar not thy false playing,
> But let not me, poor soul, know of thy straying.
> Nor do I give thee counsel to live chaste,
> But that thou wouldst dissemble, when 'tis past.
> She hath not trod awry that doth deny it.
> What madness is't to tell night's pranks by day,
> And hidden secrets openly to bewray?
>
> Be more advis'd, walk as a puritan,
> And I shall think you chaste, do what you can.
>
> *Elegy*, III. xiii. 1–7, 13–14

Marlowe's use of an Ovidian model to transform expected norms is most explicit in what is likely to have been his earliest play, *The Tragedy of Dido, Queen of Carthage*. As is typically the case, we cannot be certain about its date. Unlike the majority of Marlowe's drama, which was written for the public theatres, *Dido* was apparently performed by a company of child actors in a private theatre or at Court. Claims have been made that it was performed as early as 1587 and that its origins are in the university plays Marlowe would have been familiar with from Cambridge. *Dido* is not an inferior piece of juvenalia, though, and it has been unjustly ignored. Part of the reason for its lack of critical attention appears to stem from a continuing misrepresentation that it is nothing more than a dramatized version of Books II and IV of Virgil's *Aeneid* and that, as such, it is not particularly convincing. In fact, while using many lines directly from Virgil, the play is a calculated subversion of the heroic ideals of the *Aeneid*, an imitation which is designed to reveal differences rather than similarities with the expected model. This was perfectly usual within the Renaissance theory and practice of imitation, but Marlowe daringly chose to challenge the norms promoted by the text which was the most widely used model for heroic education in European culture. Every European vernacular was keen to have an epic, and all saw Virgil as the example they sought to emulate.

Virgil had been the poet who defined poetic propriety for Augustan Rome, and his magisterial vision of epic heroism had been challenged by Ovid – indeed it may have been Ovid's projection of alternatives to Virgilian ideals which caused him to lose favour with Augustus and earned him banishment to the Black Sea. As with most subsequent literature, the Roman classics espoused a male perspective. Virgil's *Aeneid* is the story of the wanderings of Aeneas from the fall of Troy to the establishment of a divinely ordained greater Troy in Italy. Virgil was writing a story of heroic education, a legendary history of Rome designed to depict the emergence of an ideal model for Roman civil, masculine virtue. At a particularly low point in his wanderings Aeneas arrives in Carthage, where his mother Venus and Juno conspire to have the Carthaginian Queen, Dido, fall in love with him. Aeneas, his men, and his ships are rehabilitated, but Dido wishes to have Aeneas stay and be her consort. Aeneas ultimately refuses after being reminded of his destiny and sails away leaving Dido to curse him and pronounce enmity between Carthage and Rome (Rome had completely destroyed Carthage, its main rival in the Mediterranean, about 125 years before the *Aeneid* had been written).

As Brooks Otis has skilfully shown in his *Virgil: A Study in Civilized Poetry*, one of the characteristics of the *Aeneid* is Virgil's development of a subjective style for the epic which enables the poet to speak with an authoritative narrative voice. The *Aeneid* expounds a single point of view and iterates a precise moral framework which seeks to dominate readers' responses and force accord with the narrative perspective. Thus, while Virgil is aware of the tragic aspects of Dido's love for Aeneas, and writes with feeling about her dilemma, he equally never loses sight of Aeneas' destiny and his conviction of a heroic ethos which reaches beyond individual needs. While Virgil sympathizes with Dido, he also demonstrates her passion as destructive and uncontrolled, one which Aeneas must abandon to regain his *pietas* – a type of moral faithfulness to civic demands. The broader historic and ostensibly cosmic dimension of the Dido and Aeneas episode – the need to establish Rome – is never concealed by Virgil. This grand design is revealed by Jove, who, as enthroned majesty, directs fate with an appropriately elevated grandeur.

One of the more interesting of Ovid's projects in seeking for alternative literary perspectives was to write a series of imaginary letters from heroines who have suffered as a result of their relations with heroic men. Each letter insists that readers re-imagine episodes which have established masculine success and public reputation as a result of female loss and abandonment. One such letter of Ovid's *Heroides* is from Dido to Aeneas.

As the title of Marlowe's play indicates, he is heavily indebted to this Ovidian perspective. Marlowe takes epic success with its centre of interest in the male Aeneas and translates it to a female tragedy centred on Queen Dido. In doing so the play fundamentally questions Virgil's epic organization. The first scene demonstrates immediately Marlowe's abandonment of a Virgilian ethos. The frivolous erotic banter between Jupiter and Ganymede with which the play opens undermines the god as a voice of immortal fate detailing an important destiny for Aeneas. Jupiter's invitation to Ganymede to sit upon his knees and 'Control proud Fate, and cut the thread of Time' (*Dido*, I. i. 29) demonstrates immortal irresponsibility. Ganymede, with the heaven and earth to choose from, responds by selecting only a jewel for his ear and a 'fine brooch' for his hat, illustrating the play's ridiculing of epic rhetorical grandeur and confirming the utter deflation of Jupiter as a creditable guardian of Aeneas' heroic destiny. Venus' response to Jupiter's pronouncements – 'How may I credit these thy flattering terms' (*Dido*, I. i. 109) – carries a wholly different resonance from Virgil's demonstration of Venus' lack of understanding about Jove's designs. In the *Aeneid*, Venus' inability to comprehend the demands of fate acts to confirm Jove's absolute majesty and Venus' limitations. In *Dido, Queen of Carthage*, the actions of all the immortals reduce an audience's confidence in the gods' projections of future heroic destinies.

The play's substantial achievement is that the black farce created by the gods throughout the action does not push the play into being only a sceptical satiric parody of heroic literature. The frivolity of the gods contrasts with the pathos found in the main human characters, particularly Dido. Both human tragedy and immortal folly combine to comment on the play's concern with the illusionary quality of passion – the comic elements complement and clarify the serious concerns of the drama.

In the *Aeneid*, Virgil contrasts the illusions created by Dido about her future with Aeneas against the true and (Virgil leaves us in no doubt) proper reality of Aeneas' greater destiny in Italy. In *Dido*, though, the future is abandoned and the play is constantly focused on the past. The destroyed city of Troy lingers over the actions and the characters are continuously looking backward, trying to discover ways of understanding their present from the events 'That after burnt the pride of Asia' (*Dido*, II. i. 187). Virgil presents Aeneas as the survivor who must still undergo trials before he can establish his proper destiny. Marlowe, in breaking with a credible force of cosmic destiny, presents him merely as a survivor; the dramatic concentration is on his limitation:

> And we were round environ'd with the Greeks.
> O, there I lost my wife! And, had not we
> Fought manfully, I had not told this tale.
> Yet manhood would not serve; of force we fled;
>
> *Dido*, I. i. 269-72

Aeneas is a spent force in the play. His emotional life is rooted in his Trojan past and he wants this past to become true again. As they enter Carthage, Aeneas and his companion Achates are confronted by a statue of the former Trojan king, Priam. Observing it, they share some joint memories, but Aeneas is overwhelmed by them and Achates is left bewildered by the intensity of Aeneas' desires for the past. Aeneas wishes the statue's transformation back into Priam, 'that under his conduct | We might sail back to Troy' (*Dido*, II. i. 17–18).

Marlowe's Aeneas cannot escape his memories, but he also lacks any comprehension of why the past happened the way it did. His perspective is summed up by his recognition that, though he 'fought

40

manfully . . . yet manhood would not serve'. Aeneas' first words to Dido reflect his sense of displacement: 'Sometime I was a Trojan, mighty Queen; | But Troy is not; what shall I say I am' (*Dido*, II. i. 75–6). All he can relate is his tale of the past, a story he becomes wholly absorbed by as he tells it to Dido. Despite her pleas for him to stop because of her own emotional exhaustion, he continues, possessed by the holocaust he has somehow survived.

The play proposes that Aeneas' ultimate disregard for Dido stems less from a calculated manipulation of her than from an emotional deadness to his own present. The god Hermes' insistent instructions to him to return to his quest for Italy is offered by the play not as a return to a heroic destiny but as a demand which conforms with Aeneas' vision of a world where people are battered about by forces they cannot control. He passively obeys without any need to analyse his relation with Dido. Aeneas' treatment of Dido is shoddy, but it evokes his own ruined quality.

This very unheroic Aeneas makes Dido's passion for him all the more poignant because it is so firmly anchored in illusion. Although formally prompted by Cupid's arrow, the play suggests Dido's desire for Aeneas is already rooted before his arrival, motivated by her own fascination with his Trojan legacy. As Aeneas relates Troy's downfall, Dido is overcome by an erotic response to events in which she has clearly long taken an interest. She, too, looks back with horror, yet compulsive fascination, at the Trojan holocaust. In her rage towards Aeneas as he announces his departure, she reveals how she wishes to assume a role from Troy's past – seeking a legendary quality she imagines as more compelling than her present reality, even if such a role destroys her world. She announces that she has been called a second Helen:

> So thou wouldst prove as true as Paris did,
> Would, as fair Troy was, Carthage might be sack'd,
> And I be call'd a second Helena!

> *Dido*, V. i. 146–8

Just as Aeneas' desire for the metamorphosis of Priam's statue emphasized the illusion of such hopes, so Dido's wish to become part of a destroyed past only emphasizes the illusions she tries to live by. This is very close to the tone of Ovid's *Heroides*, but Marlowe's play has substantially expanded the context for

Ovid's denunciations of Aeneas, further questioning the claims of a masculine epic ethos by having audiences witness a world where destiny and divine control are thoroughly undermined. It is a tragedy for Dido that she is obsessed with a heroic image of Aeneas which she has invented out of Trojan legend but which his dramatic presence no longer manifests. Marlowe's play, though, hints at a more general tragedy of human illusion. Subverting the Virgilian heroic ethos, *Dido, Queen of Carthage* also asks its audiences to recognize that the ideals manifested by such epics generally may be false. The norms through which idealized life may be represented, the moral didacticism of Virgil, is displaced.

Dido, Queen of Carthage appears to have been written for a company of children actors, so it may be argued that the original staging of the play was directed merely at comic deflation and parody of the epic: Dido and Aeneas, Jupiter and Ganymede, Venus and Juno being played by boys alongside the play's actual roles for children in Cupid and Ascanius might seem constructed to emphasize amusement rather than tragedy. While it is difficult to reconstruct the cultural circumstances and audience expectations of early productions, I was surprised in witnessing a recent production of *Dido* by the King's School, Canterbury, that the absurdity of Jupiter and Ganymede and the adolescent statures of Aeneas and the Trojans did not ridicule Dido's pathos but actually enhanced it. Admittedly, the girl who took the part of Dido gave a very accomplished performance (and she was, of course, a young woman not a boy), but it indicates how Marlowe's text succeeds in integrating the farcical, the darkly comic, and the more serious tragic elements of the play to create a successful dramatic whole.

The exaggeration of the Dido story in Marlowe's play in comparison with its Virgilian counterpart should be seen as an attempt to portray an alternative vision to Virgil's, to contend with the epic. At the play's end there is a sequence of destruction which provides dramatic spectacle and which focuses on the Carthaginian tragedy of Dido's violent self-immolation. Virgil, by contrast, has Dido die quietly, slowly breathing out her last, and intensely details her individual misery. Marlowe's play acts to present a familiar episode (the *Aeneid* was a central school text and its stories well known throughout England) in an unfamiliar manner. Even in what is probably his first play, Marlowe is showing his drama's capacity to merge familiar and exotic. He staged material long circulating in

Elizabethan culture but stressed its foreignness and unfamiliarity. There is much about Dido's Carthage which suggests exotic opulence, a counterpart for Cleopatra's Egypt. But, whereas in *Antony and Cleopatra* Shakespeare clearly identifies and separates a western Roman perspective from an eastern Egyptian one, in *Dido* there is only an exotic Carthage and the memory of an equally Asiatic Troy. By refusing the Virgilian perspective, Marlowe is also refusing to have the play concur with existing cultural norms about literature's role in heroic instruction. *Dido*, like the plays which follow it, generates a cultural hybridity which poses unresolved questions about the human capacity for controlled government, either of self or of nation. Marlowe sceptically interrogates literary conventions by demonstrating that the moral idealism widely felt to be generated by literary icons such as the *Aeneid* may be re-presented in morally less confident displays. As we see, though, one way Marlowe developed his critique of the claims for literature promoted by Sidney or Spenser was through aligning his art with alternatives within the classical tradition itself. One of the roots of Marlovian innovation, therefore, rested in the Renaissance practice of imitation; but, where others stressed similarities, Marlowe was fascinated by difference.

6

The World on the Stage

In 1589, the year preceding the publication of Marlowe's *Tamburlaine* and over a year since the plays had been staged, the first edition appeared of Richard Hakluyt's *The Principal Navigations, Voyages, and Discoveries of the English Nation*. This extensive collection of voyage narratives testifies to the enormous growth in England's interest in the world; Hakluyt's text contained details of virtually every corner of the earth, including Cavendish's circumnavigation of the globe (1586–8). What stands out in these narratives, however, is their interest in how money can be made. Whether in trade with the near and far east; pillage gained from the Spanish or others the world over; the discovery of previously unknown natural riches; even in the catalogues of deprivation and appalling conditions suffered in remote corners while searching for more profitable places, these accounts reveal an English perception of the world as a potential treasure house. In 1598–1600, when the expanded second edition appeared the significant word *Traffiques* was added to the title. Hakluyt celebrates a new strain in an English national spirit, the equation of mercantile success with patriotic pride. In the Epistle Dedicatory to Sir Francis Walsingham in the original 1589 edition, Hakluyt applauds a vision of a global market in which trading ventures become rhetorically elided with political conquest. Queen Elizabeth emerges both as voyager and as monarch at the centre of a world which pays tribute to her. Although lengthy, Hakluyt's vision of plentitude in commodity and space – his excitement over places formerly distant and exotic becoming incorporated into an English sphere – is worth quoting at length:

> it can not be denied, but as in all former ages, they have bene men full of activity, stirrers abroad, and searchers of the remote parts of the world, so in this most famous and peerlesse government of her most excellent Majesty, her subjects, through the speciall assistance, and blessing of God, in searching the most opposite corners of the world . . . in compassing

the vaste globe of the earth more than once, have excelled all the nations and people of the earth. For, which of the kings of this land before her Majesty, had their banners ever seen in the Caspian Sea? Which of them hath ever dealth with the Emperor of Persia, as her Majesty hath done, and obtained for her merchants large and loving privileges? who ever saw before this regiment, an English Ligier in the stately porch of the Grand Signor at Constantinople? Who ever found English consuls and agents at Tripolis in Syria, at Aleppo, at Babylon, at Balsara and which is more, whoever heard of Englishmen at Goa before now? What English ships did heretofore ever anchor in the mighty river at Plate? Pass and repass the unpassable (in former opinion) strait of Magellan, range along the coast of Chile, Peru, and all the backside of Nova Hispania, further than any Christian ever passed, traverse the mighty breath of the South Sea, land upon the Luzones in despite of the enemy, enter into alliance, amity and traffike with the princes of the Moluccas and the Isle of Java, double the famous Cape of Bona Speranza, arrive at the isle of St Helena, and last of all return home most richly lade with the commodities of China, as the subjects of this now flourishing monarchy have done?

This sense of excitement over place and the energetic acquiring of it, the rhetoric of magnitude and accumulation, are matched by Marlowe's drama. Compare Tamburlaine's mapping of his conquests at the end of the two plays which bear his name:

> Here I began to march toward Persia,
> Along Armenia and the Caspian Sea,
> And thence to Bithynia, where I took
> The Turk and his great empress prisoners.
> Then march'd I into Egypt and Arabia;
> And here, not far from Alexandria,
> Whereas the Terrene and the Red Sea meet,
> Being distant less than full a hundred leagues,
> I meant to cut a channel to them both
> That men might quickly sail to India.
> From thence to Nubia near Borno Lake,
> And so along the Aethiopian sea,
> Cutting the Tropic line of Capricorn,
> I conquer'd all as far as Zanzibar.
> Then, by the northern part of Africa,
> I came at last to Graecia, and from thence
> To Asia . . .

Which is from Scythia, where I began,
Backward and forwards near five thousand leagues.

2 Tamb. V. iii. 127–45

In a similar vein, Barabas, the Jew of Malta, is first encountered in his counting-house detailing his opulent plentitude. He compares the smaller returns gained from the Mediterranean trade of oils and wines with the extraordinary scale of riches available from the east. The difference between this latter 'traffic' and the former 'vulgar trade' is one which, he suggests, distinguishes 'men of judgement'. His vision conflates the wealth gathered by a merchant with political exchanges between states, noting how kings require the money generated by merchants. Money is power.

> Give me the merchants of the Indian mines,
> That trade in metal of the purest mould;
> The wealthy Moor, that in the eastern rocks
> Without control can pick his riches up,
> And in his house heap pearl like pebble stones,
> Receive them free, and sell them by the weight!
> Bags of fiery opals, sapphires, amethysts,
> Jacints, hard topaz, grass-green emeralds,
> Beauteous rubies, sparkling diamonds,
> And seld-seen costly stones of so great price,
> As one of them, indifferently rated,
> And of a carat of this quantity,
> May serve, in peril of calamity,
> To ransom great kings from captivity.
> This is the ware wherein consists my wealth.

Jew, I. i. 19–33

Marlowe's language matches this inflationary vision, building in its accumulating images, its lists of exotic places or gems, a picture of excess which combines space and wealth. Tamburlaine conquers an Asia and Africa overflowing with riches. He and his followers desire territory in order to acquire splendour; to rule is to possess abundance. A catalogue of conquest allows Tamburlaine and his followers to 'glut us with the dainties of the world' – even gold and precious stones become consumables for them (*2 Tamb.* I. iii. 220–5). Tamburlaine would reduce the world to a map so that he can possess and name it after himself and Zenocrate (*1 Tamb.* IV. iv. 80–8); he would reduce the globe to encompass it, so that he can be readily seen to possess it. Barabas's mercantile voyages through far-flung kingdoms are to 'inclose | Infinite riches in a little room' (*Jew*, I. i. 35-6). Accumulation allows the transgression of spatial organizations. Barabas's phraseology here parallels the use of metaphysical paradox employed by contemporary devotional poets to record the wonders of Christ's Incarnation. When the Turks in *The Jew of Malta* return to the island, and the governor, knowing they come for promised tribute, asks 'What wind drives you thus into Malta-road?', his question seems dramatically designed to give prominence to the Basso's answer: 'The wind that bloweth all the world, besides, | Desire of gold' (*Jew*, III. v. 2–4).

Marlowe's drama explores the possibilities generated by abundance – in land, wealth, knowledge, and power – in four plays: the two parts of *Tamburlaine*, *The Jew of Malta*, and *Doctor Faustus*. His approach differs in each one; yet it is important to note how all these plays participate in visions of imaginative excess. Just as Hakluyt's *Voyages*, Marlowe's plays reflect a sense of expansion being experienced throughout Elizabethan society. The Ditchley Portrait of Queen Elizabeth, dating, too, from about 1590, shows her dressed as the imperial virgin standing on the globe, her feet upon England, as though (like Tamburlaine's desire to reduce the world to a map) she ruled because the land itself was literally as well as metaphorically smaller than her majesty.

Hakluyt's vision of Elizabeth as global monarch was without foundation in actuality. As even a cursory reading of his collection of narratives reveals, most of these English 'discoveries' more readily acknowledge that the English were rather late in the field among such European endeavours. The most ambitious of English voyages of exploration were to discover trade routes that might allow them to outflank their established Spanish or Portuguese competitors; many voyages were also organized to harass the well-established outposts of these countries by acquiring plunder. What Hakluyt's celebration reveals, though, is that reality and fantasy were closely associated when it came to representing the world to Elizabethan readers. Sir Walter Ralegh's 1596 account of his voyage to Guiana, for example, represents this tropical region of South America as a fertile classical pastoral paradise populated by Indians who are all desirous to be Queen Elizabeth's subjects and where incalculable amounts of gold are waiting just over the mountains!

The first play of *Tamburlaine* is the most emphatic demonstration of Marlowe's participation in this Elizabethan rhetoric of opportunity, presenting a world of excess and inflated possibilities. Although the two plays were printed together from their earliest edition in 1590 as Parts I and II of the same work, they seem to have been conceived independently, the second being generated from the stage success of the first. Certainly, the first play is an unwavering depiction of the energy and successful self-fashioning of Tamburlaine and his followers in their unchecked conquest of the Middle East, revealing a more uniform tone and singular dramatic purpose than the second. The first play is Marlowe's most unhindered celebration of this strange mixture of fantasy in ostensibly real locations which can be noted in much contemporary travel-writing. It demonstrates the east as a site of abundance – of riches and tyranny, of opulence and cruelty, of the compelling and the terrifying. It is noteworthy that this first play presents the Asia in which Tamburlaine launches his cycle of conquest as decadent, effeminate, undefended, and available for spoil. Far more than the second play, it is a vision of alterity for an English audience which stages excess and opportunity in unsurpassed magnificence.

One of Marlowe's sources of information on Tamburlaine was George Whetstone's 1586 book *The English Myrror*. As the rest of its title – *Wherein all estates may behold the Conquests of Envy* – suggests, Whetstone's book was ostensibly designed to demonstrate how the maintenance of a social and political mean is desirable (something he claims Elizabeth excels at). His tract is a collection of observations on the extremities and, thus for Whetstone, inevitable failures of despotic tyrannies, of which Tamburlaine's is one. One of the features of these usurpatious regimes which Whetstone is particularly appalled by is their reliance on the complicity of the common people in the overthrowing of 'famous and prudent government'. The consequence is that empires such as those ruled by the Turk, the Sophy (the Persian Shah), and Tamburlaine have 'neither will nor capacity to cherish vertue, learning and worthy enterprises', things which are 'the beauty and strength of a good commonwealth'. Whetstone's message to 'all estates' – the configuration of existing social classes – is to remain content with their position within English society.

Whetstone's illustrative use of Tamburlaine could not be further from the design of the first of Marlowe's plays on him. The play

enacts the rise of a Sycthian shepherd (the Scythians were synony-
mous with barbarism in the ancient world) to become ruler of a large
part of the globe. As we saw above, one of the features which some
of the City of London élite disliked about the Elizabethan theatre
was that it was seen as promoting ideas of instant rank and wealth
to its audiences. *Tamburlaine* is a vision of a dynamic force in a
decadent world in which intrinsic merit (interpreted in militaristic
terms of might, endeavour, and endurance) is shown to bring success.
Tamburlaine, as he announces to Zenocrate, daughter of the Egyptian Sultan, will show that he is a true aristocrat, possessing a nobility
defined through achievement not birth – 'I am a lord, for so my
deeds shall prove, | And yet a shepherd by my parentage' (*1 Tamb.*
I. ii. 34–5). His deeds do demonstrate his ability to exercise power,
a reversal of an Elizabethan cultural convention which proposed that
only those properly born could exercise true government. It is worth
comparing Tamburlaine with Shakespeare's rebellious figure of Jack
Cade in 2 *Henry VI*, a play which probably also dates from the late
1580s. While dramatizing Cade's rebellion so as to offer a powerful
condemnation of aristocratic claims, Shakespeare adopts the more
familiar display of this social challenge from below as generating
disorder. Cade is an acute critic, but the grotesquerie in which his
rebellion manifests itself also makes the potential of his succeeding
(or of an audience wanting him to) unlikely. In contrast, Tamburlaine
in the first play is supremely self-controlled. Indeed, the most uneasy
aspect of his absolute control of events is that he is unrelenting.
Instead of being different from the nobility through the limitations
of his birth, Tamburlaine excels them in the qualities they should
possess. As important, Marlowe's defiance of convention which
linked character to birth is extended to Tamburlaine's followers –
'these, that seem but silly country swains', Tamburlaine announces
to Zenocrate about his men at the start of their ascent to power and
riches, 'May have the leading of so great an host | As with their
weight shall make the mountains quake' (*1 Tamb.* I. ii. 47–9). Part of
the unsettling excitement of the first of the Tamburlaine plays –
particularly within the conventions of Elizabethan theatre – is that
this prediction is exactly what is dramatically fulfilled. The play ends
with Tamburlaine making a truce with the world and rewarding his
followers. Rather than descending into a spectacle of barbaric
disorder, Tamburlaine proffers the establishment of a new order. His
own crowning of Zenocrate as Queen of Persia symbolizes the union

of his masculine military enterprise with the teaming wealth of the feminine east:

> And now, my lords and loving followers,
> That purchas'd kingdoms by your martial deeds,
> Cast off your armour, put on scarlet robes,
> Mount up your royal places of estate,
> Environed with troops of noblemen,
> And there make laws to rule your provinces.
>
> *1 Tamb.* V. ii. 461–6

Everything in the first of the Tamburlaine plays works to confirm his vision of himself as an unchecked figure of abundance, a generator of plentitude offering wealth and power to his followers or destruction to his opposers. There is no middle ground with Tamburlaine; he is a personage of absolutes and recognizes himself as such:

> I hold the Fates bound fast in iron chains,
> And with my hand turn Fortune's wheel about;
> And sooner shall the sun fall from his sphere
> Than Tamburlaine be slain or overcome.
>
> *1 Tamb.* I. ii. 174–7

The action of the play represents the enactment of Tamburlaine's vision and its dramatic events are focused around moments where others either comply with his self-representation or oppose him.

For those that acknowledge the plentitude that Tamburlaine offers them, there appears not only material wealth but emotional rapture. Tamburlaine is a figure of exotic enticement, he supplies a sense of excess, of possibilities which exceed those previously available. It is not so much that Tamburlaine represents anything new in his desires: the play is filled with figures who want or believe they possess the power and abundance Tamburlaine strives for – Cosroe or Bajazeth the Turkish Emperor, for instance. They, however, imagine their right to possession derives through adherence to an old order which marks them as traditional inheritors: they belong to a courtly class. What Tamburlaine offers is a plentitude available to all who join with him; he generates possibilities for all his subscribers. As Usumcasnae reveals, one of the things that attracts Tamburlaine's followers is the potential for social reversals. They shall become rulers, the rulers shall now be slaves:

> And kingdoms at the least we all expect,
> Besides the honour in assured conquests,
> Where kings shall crouch unto our conquering swords,
> And hosts of soldiers stand amaz'd at us,
> When with their fearful tongues they shall confess,
> These are the men that all the world admires.
>
> *1 Tamb.* I. ii. 218–23.

Significantly, the play shows how this vision also entices figures whose sympathies ostensibly should remain with the forces ranged against Tamburlaine. Theridamas – the Persian captain sent to destroy him – or Zenocrate are compellingly attracted to Tamburlaine. In an extraordinary scene Tamburlaine convinces Theridamas to abandon the effeminate Persian emperor. What makes their exchange so notable is that, despite being filled with promises of wealth and power, its style and language are those of a love scene. Tamburlaine is attracted to the majesty he sees in Theridamas, Theridamas to 'nature's pride and richest furniture' (*1 Tamb.* I. ii. 155), which he instantly observes in Tamburlaine. The scene concludes with Theridamas capitulating to Tamburlaine as though concluding a marriage rather than a joint alliance:

> Won with thy words and conquer'd with thy looks,
> I yield myself, my men and horse to thee,
> To be partaker of thy good or ill
> As long as life maintains Theridamas.
>
> *1 Tamb.* I. ii. 228–31

Similarly Zenocrate overpoweringly wants to 'live and die with Tamburlaine' (*1 Tamb.* III. ii. 25). When Agydas, one of the Median lords attending her, tries to persuade her to disown him – reminding her that she is previously contracted to a true aristocrat, the king of Arabia, and that Tamburlaine is 'vile and barbarous' – Zenocrate reveals that what troubles her is not Tamburlaine's inferiority but her own, that she feels herself unworthy of his love. This exchange, which Tamburlaine overhears, concludes with him lovingly leading Zenocrate off and Agydas being forced to kill himself. The whole episode enacts in small what the play recounts about what happens on the battlefield. Characters are given the opportunity to recognize and respond to Tamburlaine's appeal or to reject him: there is reward or death.

Marlowe's presentation of Tamburlaine in this first play is not an unproblematic celebration, of course. The action increasingly presents him in an undecided fashion. His lengthy eloquent meditation on the rapture he feels at Zenocrate's beauty and the means by which he realizes 'virtue' which is the 'sum of glory | And fashions men with true nobility' (1 Tamb. V. ii. 127–8) is surrounded by his pitiless ordering of the destruction of Damascus (despite Zenocrate's pleading for its salvation) and his harsh treatment of the former Turkish emperor Bajazeth. Tamburlaine's self-definition of virtue constantly clashes with convention and, despite the allurement of his poetry, a gap is created between the rhetorical construction of his actions and the spectacle – and consequences – of those actions.

Tamburlaine in both plays presents himself as the 'Scourge of God'. The meaning of this is not clear: he may be acting as an instrument of God in chastising existing human orders or he may be demonstrating human savagery in deliberately wrecking a providential order of reward and punishment which God has provided to govern humanity's best interest. The first play of Tamburlaine, in particular, leaves this role uncertain, largely through setting the action in an exotic east where Christian concerns are touched on only tangentially. Marlowe's play represents similar challenges to those posed by English encounters with previously unknown regions. Unlike the Spanish, the English were not overly concerned with religious conversion of either known heathens such as the Turk or the newly encountered peoples of their 'discoveries'. It is plausible that a response to Tamburlaine's world among its first audiences would be similar to the perception of later English buccaneers about their conduct in plundering their way around the Pacific: 'there is no God this side of Cape Horn.' Instead of an area of moral dilemma, Tamburlaine's eastern empire offered English readers or spectators the enticement of the exotic, where conventional barriers and categories of discrimination could be abandoned in pursuit of splendour and reward. Certainly, one of the important models for dealing with distant lands – the hugely popular fourteenth-century text Mandeville's Travels – had helped establish the perception that the further you went from civilization's centre the less and less godly the territories you encountered. The more exotic the land, the less the expectation that English norms for godly conduct applied, and this created either anxiety or opportunity (or both!) depending on the circumstances.

The first play of *Tamburlaine* concentrates on dramatizing an exotic difference whose unresolved quality recognizes its audiences' desires for it to remain alluringly unfamiliar. As the responses of Theridamas and Zenocrate show, the play's language and the actions it suggests are erotically charged, and, like erotica, this drama compels and repulses, combines impossible fantasy and suggestive opportunity, in quite complex ways. The play reflects aspects which are enticing (such as the possibilities for wealth and position), yet resists becoming a document for English social change by remaining firmly settled on the remote. Unlike the didactic potentials of fictional other places found in texts such as Thomas More's *Utopia*, the first *Tamburlaine* play participates more readily in the fragmentary and discontinuous representations found in contemporary voyage narratives. As Hakluyt's own account of how he came 'to prosecute . . . that kind of literature' reveals, there was an appetite for the exotic among readers, armchair voyagers, or witnesses of dramatic spectacles that offered contained versions of exciting alterity, ones displayed in the controlled spaces of theatres – places of possibilities that were simultaneously both present and distant.

The second *Tamburlaine* play has a different quality from the first. Confronting the newly defeated Turkish powers, Tamburlaine reprimands them for not recognizing him for what he is:

> these terrors and these tyrannies
> (If tyrannies war's justice ye repute),
> I execute, enjoin'd me from above,
> To scourge the pride of such as Heaven abhors;
> Nor am I made arch-monarch of the world,
> Crown'd and invested by the hand of Jove,
> For deeds of bounty or nobility;
> But since I exercise a greater name,
> The Scourge of God and terror of the world,
> I must apply myself to fit those terms,
> In war, in blood, in death, in cruelty,
> And plague such peasants as resist in me
> The power of Heaven's eternal majesty.

> 2 *Tamb.* IV. i. 148–60

Whereas the nature of what Tamburlaine represents in Part I is unresolved, Part II diminishes his self-fashioning will. In this second play, Tamburlaine becomes an instrument for God to scourge those whom 'Heaven abhors', particularly shown to be Europe's traditional enemy, the Turks. At the beginning of the play Orcanes, one of the Turkish kings, presents a detailed description of intended bloody conquest which matches Tamburlaine's rhetoric of excessive blood-letting (2 *Tamb.* I. i. 25–44). The difference is that his catalogue of desired carnage is directed against Christian Europe. One of the other Turkish kings notes that this conquest will have to be postponed until they have dealt with Tamburlaine, who (of course!) defeats them and prevents their ravaging of Europe. The first play's greater unease about how Tamburlaine's destructive power could be allowed in an ostensibly providentially governed world is thus contained by the second's reference to a Christian God who organizes things to allow heathens to destroy one another in order to prevent their terror from reaching the west.

This is a substantial change of emphasis, and it is matched by a difference in the second play's presentation of Tamburlaine. His might, power, and sense of absolutism remain – though he has less of the poetic eloquence which denotes him in the first play; the Tamburlaine of the second play, however, is a much more conventional tyrant, controlling not so much with the help of a charged eroticism but with an unfeeling cruelty. His murder of his son who refuses to participate in the carnage of battles presents a figure close to a conventional view of the corrupted eastern despot. The execution of the Babylonian governor similarly has a savage quality which gives it a more distasteful tone than even the first play's slaughter of the Damascus virgins.

This different emphasis does not appear merely accidental. An episode which well illustrates a change of design in the second play is the encounter between Theridamas and Olympia, the wife of the captain of Balsera who dies in the defence of his city. Olympia kills her own son and looks to kill herself rather than fall into the hands of Tamburlaine's troops. She is prevented by Theridamas, who becomes captivated by her and wants to make her his queen. In many respects this parallels Tamburlaine's capture of Zenocrate in the first play. There, however, Zenocrate becomes entranced by Tamburlaine, and even the death of her previously intended husband, the king of Arabia, and the destruction of Damascus did not cause her to abandon her passion. Olympia is not so won over. Despite Theridamas's attempts to woo her with promises of love and riches, she remains resolved in her wish to die to be with her husband and son. This provokes Theridamas to threats of rape, and only by trickery does she manage to get him to kill her. What in Zenocrate's and Tamburlaine's case was a magnificent example of the first play's compelling exoticism, in the second play becomes an undermining of the opulence and eroticism of Tamburlaine's empire. Olympia's maintenance of the classic moral position of the faithful wife exposes the violence and savagery of Theridamas 'I must and will be pleas'd, and you shall yield' (2 *Tamb*. IV. iii. 53).

My discussion of the two *Tamburlaine* plays has emphasized their differences, but from their first publication in 1590 they have been viewed as a unit. Much in both plays supports continuities between them, but this has tended to mask an observation of their differences. By seeing them as yoked indissolubly together it can be argued that the second play merely highlights developing concerns of the first play, showing Tamburlaine's gradual display of more savage elements previously masked in earlier scenes. In a similar vein, it can be proposed that the wonder generated by the first play is not sufficiently revoked in the second and that Tamburlaine's significance remains as unresolved at the conclusion of the second play as it was at the end of the first. Certainly, there have been difficulties in categorizing what the sum of the parts of *Tamburlaine* is designed to present since the plays' first publication. The title-page of the 1590 edition describes them as 'two tragicall discourses', whereas they were entered into the Stationer's Register as 'commicall discourses'. A comic mode is probably more appropriate to the first play, where the tragic may be seen as more suitable to the second. While it is the case that, once both parts were in circulation, they appear to have been acted together as well as combined in textual form; this should not, however, deter us from recognizing the first play's initial independence and its difference from the second. The relation between the two parts of *Tamburlaine* joins the two versions of *Doctor Faustus* in demonstrating the difficulties in trying to understand the relations of texts to culture, as well as the limits of later interpretations, when dealing with a drama which is not available in an authorially approved stabilized form.

7

Types of Characters

One of the features *Tamburlaine* shares with Marlowe's other drama is its presentation of characters as players of designated roles:

> since I exercise a greater name,
> The Scourge of God and terror of the world,
> I must apply myself to fit those terms

> 2 *Tamb.* IV. i. 155–7

Dramatic figures in these plays are vehicles for actions, they are not psychologically complex. In Marlowe's drama there is no real interest in demonstrating individual subjectivities through intimating an interior life. The dominance of the realistic novel with its emphasis on psychology in characterization has made many modern readers see interiority as an essential component in sophisticated literary writing, but such a concept was alien to early modern writers. Marlowe's drama eschews the illusion of realism in characterization. Dramatic characters are emblematic figures – not in some simple and crude sense but in keeping with an idea that identities are linked to determined roles.

Catherine Belsey, among a number of recent critics, has argued that Renaissance drama mixes the relatively clear significations of what characters 'meant' in the medieval morality tradition's delineations of vice and virtue with a more complicated 'illusionist' drama of realism, one concerned with a greater plurality of possible meanings. While there are merits in considering Shakespearian drama in this fashion, Marlowe's plays are more concerned to amend the morality tradition's representation of recognized values through depicting challenging figures in uncertain cultural environments, characters who remain puzzling because the codes of meanings they project no longer belong to secure norms for interpreting them. The complexity of Tamburlaine, Faustus, Barabas, Edward, or Isabella rests not in their being more like 'real people' than a previous morality tradition, but in their challenging significations – the emblematic codes which they exhibit – which question previous structures of knowledge and belief. Where a dramatic morality tradition participated in a cultural hegemony and relied on known representations to clarify its meanings, Marlowe's drama testifies to cultural alternatives, a loss of hegemony. It was the recognition of a more complex but less secure world order which provoked Marlovian drama, and the plays themselves contributed to an undermining of hegemony through, if nothing else, their demonstration that insecurity of meaning can be aesthetically involving.

If the first *Tamburlaine* play illustrates Marlowe's alluring new possibilities as enticing, *Doctor Faustus* offers them in a troublesome context. Like Tamburlaine, Faustus presents his life as a project of conquest seeking to overthrow existing orders. Where Tamburlaine rises through military conquests of territory which bring him power, Faustus – starting, too, from humble origins – seeks to achieve his goals through an exercise of knowledge. Interestingly, Faustus's self-projection maintains a noticeable masculine cast, sharing Tamburlaine's association of aspiration as belonging to male prowess – 'Learn thou of Faustus manly fortitude', he tells Mephostophilis, 'And scorn those joys thou never shall possess' (*Faust*. I. iii. 86–7). The play opens with Faustus projecting a conquest of traditional academic disciplines whose function he sees as leading him to material wealth. He considers and dispenses with logic, medicine, law, and divinity before he arrives at necromancy:

> O, what a world of profit and delight,
> Of power, of honour, of omnipotence,
> Is promised to the studious artizan!
> All things that move between the quiet poles
> Shall be at my command. Emperors and kings
> Are but obeyed in their several provinces.
> Nor can they raise the wind or rend the clouds.
> But his dominion that exceeds in this
> Stretcheth as far as doth the mind of men.
>
> *Faust*. I. i. 52–60

Tamburlaine's dramatic success rests on the lack of a credible challenge to his material secularism. Faustus's world is very different. His 'power' is dependent on his acknowledgement of higher authority in Satan (and by implication God), a superior force whose dramatic presence compromises Faustus's rhetorical assertions – for example, his suggestion that he can transform hell or heaven into Elysium, or his attempts to use logical sophistry to debate with Mephostophilis about the quality of hell. Faustus may argue that, because he has never seen God, and therefore has no understanding of Mephostophilis's definition of hell as the absence of God, that he inhabits a 'hell' which is a perfectly satisfactory place to be from his perspective and, thus, not really 'hell' (*Faust*. I. iii. 55–89; I. v. 130–42). This logical and linguistic sophistry is confronted by the dramatic acutality of Mephostophilis: 'I am an instance to prove the contrary' (*Faust*. I. v. 139). Faustus's delight in engaging in such displays of words indicates less his intellectual abilities than a type of adolescent refusal to recognize the powers he has invoked, a position made poignant in his continuing insistence on academic speculation in the face of sinister presences: 'Think'st thou that Faustus is so fond to imagine | That after this life there is any pain?' (*Faust*. I. v. 136–7). Although one of Elizabethan England's accepted beliefs about the devil was that you could not trust what he says (and, therefore, all the 'facts' Mephostophilis states may be lies), the play is intent on giving an aura of plausibility to the devil's power. Mephostophilis is quite ready to tell Faustus that his 'magic' has only conjured devils because his abjuring of Christianity brought them searching for Faustus's soul, there was no inherent power in his necromancy. While Faustus may imagine that he is the master of a theatre of spectacle under his control, the action shows him to be a player in a theatre controlled by darker forces.

It is, though, *Doctor Faustus*'s insistence on the theatrical which complicates the play. Ostensibly a controlled morality drama – set off by a chorus which in the play's prologue and conclusion informs the audience what they are supposed to be witnessing – the drama we actually experience refuses this controlling structure through its own layers of theatrical playing. It is as though the devil's theatre which controls Faustus's is itself ordered by the demands of a secular theatre – the need for entertainment which the play seeks for its audiences. The seriousness of the 'meaning of Faustus' as articulated by the chorus is compromised by the disorders generated by the demands for theatrical spectacle throughout.

As Mikhail Bakhtin's influential work on comic transgression – particularly his ideas about carnival – in early modern culture has proposed, the comic can parody the tragic, revealing a different and contradictory reality from the lofty one prompted by serious literary genres. While claiming to be a tragedy, *Doctor Faustus*, in either of its versions, is filled with comedy – whether in the disruptive pranks of Faustus and Mephostophilis on the Pope; the servant figures who try to imitate Faustus; or even in Lucifer's own spectacle of the seven deadly sins, who are far from threatening figures! When two ostlers get hold of Faustus's books to conjure, they see the benefits of magic as enabling them to get free drink and sex with the kitchen maid, Nan Spit (it is worth noting that Faustus's first and last requests to Mephostophilis involve sex). For this transgression of serious conjuring, Mephostophilis angrily tells them he shall transform them into an ape and dog. Their reaction, though, is of pleasure – they will be able to get food more easily. Mephostophilis's terrors are seen as rewards, his threatening presence is ludicrously undermined. The Satanic quest in reducing higher beings to lower ones, turning them to beasts in this case, is ridiculed by the condition of ostlers who imagine themselves below the level of the beasts they serve. The hierarchies of hell or heaven are confronted in the debasement and consequent ridiculing of supernatural powers by these clowns who propose different conditions of life from the ones supposedly present in the more serious playing for souls.

In his revelling or in his role as an obliging master of shows for the emperor or fellow scholars, Faustus shares a great deal with the 'clowns' of the play. Rather than separating tragic and comic, serious and farcical, Marlowe's drama portrays their linkage and, thus, their limiting effects on one another. In one respect *Doctor Faustus* parodies the more serious concern about souls which is a central feature of organized religion; the play transgresses the moral confines of an earlier drama which had acted as an adjunct to religious teaching and reveals religion's limitations. In another respect, though, Faustus's selling of his soul so that he can gain twenty-four years of entertainment with himself in the starring role also offers the unsettling proposal that there might be areas outside this composed theatre which are far less pleasant. While it is possible to see this latter conclusion reductively asserting something similar to the older moralities (attempts at transgressions of higher orders are only temporary so do not place much store by them), what is represented also contains the elements of a deeper scepticism. Despite opportunities to imagine roles and live illusions (and this might include organized religion) in a human 'theatre of the world', what exists beyond this space may refuse our illusionary constructions. The final chorus tells us 'Faustus is gone' and we are enjoined to 'Regard his hellish fall', but, significantly, we do not literally see this fall into hell. What actually awaits Faustus beyond the limits of his allotted play-time remains unknown (this is an aspect much more apparent in the 1604 A text of the play).

What happens when heaven or hell removes its mask? The play modifies its tragic vision of powerful supernatural forces who use humanity as their theatre of combat with a more playful vision of acting participated in by the supernatural as well as humanity. In its emphasis on fashioning various theatres within the play – there are a large number of variations on the play-within-the-play motif in *Faustus* – Marlowe's drama complicates the limits of where we should see theatre ending and reality beginning. The real and the illusionary construction of Faustus's time (twenty-four years or twenty-four hours or two and a half hours in performance) become fused and, as a result, open to transformations either into abstract but meaningful symbol (for example, as the short space allotted humanity) or into meaningless fragments in which to perform escapades. Similarly, the chorus's attempt to have the play display representative and contained moral emblems only acts to reveal the artifice of such containing structures. Virtually every character in the play seeks to organize contrived spectacle, sights which transgress distinctions between illusion and reality. This apparent desire to create and then control theatre – shared as much by Lucifer as by Faustus – acts to question the nature of what is being made. As the constructions and limits of theatre within the play are made problematic, so their ramifications for 'theatres' outside the play are implicit. The social, political, or other cultural orders which attempt to give significance to actions in the real world, which try to show events and characters as possessing comprehensible meanings – for example, as dramatizations or emblems of justice or criminality, godly or ungodly behaviour – may themselves begin to seem pieces of suspiciously contrived theatre, possible illusions. Unlike a morality drama which justifies 'playing' because it shows how life should be conducted in reality, Marlowe's drama offers a theatricality which demonstrates how unknown the reality which lies beyond the realm of the play may be and our helplessness in trying to resolve its nature. The play proposes that to discover the final truth about Faustus, whether it is comic, tragic, or both, we shall have to wait until all forms of theatre are concluded.

The Jew of Malta is also a play replete with self-conscious theatricality. Barabas, the principal character, is both an accomplished dissembler (as he keeps reminding us) and a brilliant organizer of spectacle. We witness various mini-dramas he organizes among figures who let themselves be destructively drawn into his tissue of deceit; we also hear recounted a number of similar antics. In a striking exchange between Barabas and his newly acquired Turkish slave Ithamore, the two detail a catalogue of various cruelties practised on Christians, a compendium which illustrates many of the racist fears circulating in early modern England about Jews and Moors (*Jew*, II. iii. 172–220): 'We are villains both, | Both circumcised. We hate Christians both,' Barabas announces (*Jew*, II. iii. 219–20) – as though criminality, hatred of Christianity, and something which physically marks off their races are interchangeable, easy-distinguishing features of Jews and Turks. It is significant that Marlowe's Jew has the name of the murderer, robber, and figure of sedition whom the Jews preferred to see released so that Christ could be crucified (Luke 23: 18–19; John 19).

Like *Faustus*, *The Jew of Malta* offers itself as a framed tableau in which to witness suggestive actions. But, where *Faustus*'s chorus tried to provide a conventional moral framework in which to encompass the play's action, *The Jew* is presented by Machevill, a reductive stage figure of the Italian political theorist and historian Machiavelli. In Elizabethan England Machiavelli was popularly known through his (undeserved) reputation as an ungodly, diabolical Italian, a figure of deception who was against all morality. 'I count religion but a childish toy,' Marlowe's Machevill announces in his Prologue; 'Many will talk of title to a crown: | What right had Caesar to the empery?' (*Jew*, Prologue, 14, 18–19). The Prologue thus offers the expectation of 'the tragedy of a Jew' which will show how the Machiavellian Barabas uses underhand methods to secure wealth and meets an unfortunate end.

Marlowe's use of Machevill as a partial framing device for the play is complex. Where many might imagine him to be recommending Barabas in an approving way (a reversal of Aristotle's suggestion that the principal figure of a tragedy should be fundamentally a good character whose destruction an audience would regret), what we witness is Barabas's ultimate fall through being insufficiently Machiavellian to sustain himself. As the Prologue proposes, by reading Machiavelli many have become Pope but 'when they cast me off, | Are poison'd by my climbing followers' (12–13). Barabas reaches what he considers the height of his power in 'selling' Malta back to the Christians after the Turks have made him governor of the island. 'Why, is not this | A kingly kind of trade, to purchase towns | By treachery, and sell 'em by deceit?' (*Jew*, V. v. 49–51), Barabas excitedly exclaims, believing he has fulfilled the equation of trade with political might that he celebrates in his opening speech. His supposed triumph, though, immediately precedes the Christians reneging on their arrangements with him and arranging his downfall. Despite ever more complicated pieces of stage management to reduce his enemies who look to gain from him, Barabas is unable to sustain himself in the presence of a more powerful Machiavellianism practised by the play's Christians.

Although participating in a contemporary European anti-Semitism in its portrayal of Barabas, the play complicates its demonstration of Jewish deceit by presenting no alternative systems of values. Barabas is driven by the same desire for gold which motivates all the play's characters, whether Christians, Turks, or Jews. The Turkish design on Malta is to gain tribute money; the Christians tax the Jews to pay this money and then realize they can keep this wealth and refuse to pay the tribute on the expectation of Spanish support. Although rhetorics of honour, of religious integrity, or of national pride are used to justify actions, other remarks or contradictory courses of action by the races represented in the play make explicit their shared underlying motivation for material wealth – even Lodowick, the suitor of Abigail, speaks of her as a gem to be purchased. Barabas is the same as other figures in seeking material opportunity; his principal difference is that he does not mask the end of his motivations, while the others hide behind a language of religious-national proprieties. Ferneze, the Christian governor of the island, justifies his financial penalties against the Jews because they are infidels: 'For through our sufferance of your hateful lives, | Who stand accursed in the sight of heaven, | These taxes and afflictions are befall'n' (*Jew*, I. ii. 66-8). In outwitting Barabas and Turks at the play's end, Ferneze asks that 'due praise be given, | Neither to Fate nor Fortune, but to Heaven' (*Jew*, V. v. 130-1); it is clear, though, that this assertion is a classic demonstration of Machiavellian subterfuge (Machiavelli claimed in *The Prince* that it was better for a ruler to appear to have virtue than actually to inhibit his freedom of action by genuinely being virtuous). The end of *The Jew of Malta* is certainly not designed as a legitimate assertion of Christian providence. In *The Massacre at Paris* the villainous Guise has a long speech which reveals his view of the expediency of religion in furthering desires for power and wealth. His public self-presentation of himself as a defender of Catholicism is simply a mask:

> My policy hath fram'd religion.
> Religion: *O Diabole!* . . . | To think a word of such a simple sound,
> Of so great matter should be made the ground!
>
> *Massacre*, I. ii. 65–6; 68–9

The Jew of Malta reveals Barabas a poor Machiavellian because he imagines that his blunt self-appraisal of his policy is better than the hypocrisies practised by the Christians. Barabas ultimately wants the status and power of a ruler without the need to govern his territory publically; he seeks an unimpeded privacy for his wealth. For him, Machiavellianism is a means to an end (the getting of riches); his ultimate desire is to appear no more than he actually is – a thoroughly successful merchant. The play reveals, though, that proper policy rests with appearing to pursue principles aimed at the social good when actually pursuing utterly different ends. The socially approved image must be maintained; this is the foremost requirement of the successful Machiavellian, as revealed in *The Jew of Malta*. Ferneze's final speech reflects one aspect that the reputation of Malta enjoyed in Marlowe's time – its successful self-defence against an overwhelming Turkish invasion in 1565. Ferneze's speech hints at the island's reputation as defender of Christendom against Islam, but the play demonstrates this reputation grounded not in Christian virtue but in greed and subterfuge. Malta, Ferneze's closing remarks reveal, can be made to appear something it is not – a consummation of Machiavellian aims.

The theatricality of *The Jew of Malta*, with its displays of role-playing in pursuit of material gains, shows a much more contained Marlovian scepticism than *Doctor Faustus* and a far less challenging vision in comparison with that displayed in the first *Tamburlaine* play. Although set in a distant location, its exoticism is far more restrained than Tamburlaine's remoter empire and, rather than displaying encounters with supernatural forces whose designs lurked uncomfortably close for most people in Marlowe's England, the world of *The Jew* exhibits a foreignness with much more pre-defined qualities. Marlowe's Malta is the dangerous 'other', not a compelling exotic location but a more geographically and politically comprehended place.

A text such as Whetstone's *English Myrror* (which Marlowe used for *Tamburlaine*) defines the Turks as the chief enemies of Christians, but it is characteristic of its age in spending as much of its energies describing the ungodliness of Roman Catholics, the perceived persecutors of the 'true witnesses of the Gospel'. The Pope is identified as the Antichrist at war with Protestant saints, a view to be found countlessly repeated in Tudor Protestant propaganda. In Elizabethan England, while it was theoretically better to be any type of Christian than to be a Turk or Jew, in practice popular Protestantism (which was particularly strong in London) saw Turk, Jew, and Catholic as all subscribing to diabolical endeavours, with the major difference that Turk and Jew were distant heathens (Jews had been banished from England in the Middle Ages) while the Catholic menace was imagined as closely impinging on the nation's security. The second *Tamburlaine* play restrains the challenge of Tamburlaine's destructive success by suggesting that his killing of heathens keeps the Turks from Christian Europe. Nevertheless, one of the play's extensive sub-plots presents the deceptions of the Christian Hungarians in launching an attack on the Turks after they have sworn not to, an attack which results in the Christians' destruction. *Tamburlaine's* Hungarians share a great deal with the Maltese of *The Jew*, but we should not for a moment imagine that Marlowe's first audiences identified with either group. Both represented the untrustworthy Catholic forces which were potential threats to Protestant Europe. If the Turks destroy the Hungarians and then are themselves destroyed by Tamburlaine's armies, this could be witnessed as evidence of how the communities of God's 'true saints' (the Protestants) are defended by providential actions which cause heathens and traitors to God to decimate one another. In *The Jew of Malta*, an identification of the Maltese with the forces of the Antichrist is enhanced by their alliance with the Spanish. In post-Armada England of the 1590s, the Spanish were perceived as the chief Catholic menace and identified with the Antichrist's worst excesses: 'I rejoice that a Spaniard outwent an Italian in revenge', gloats Vasques at the end of a catalogue of cruel deaths in Ford's *'Tis Pity She's a Whore*.

Barabas's role in *The Jew of Malta* exposes the hypocrisies which English Protestantism imagined were exhibited by Catholicism, and part of the play's contemporary popularity with audiences is likely to have been that it represented these reductive views in a clever web of stage-managed exposés. In many respects, the play parallels the preoccupations of current TV mini-series or bestsellers about the rich and glamorous: there is a reasonably exotic location which allows a large number of figures to have walk-ons; there is family strife involving cross-racial teenage love; there is a great deal of time spent on getting or keeping wealth on a scale vastly in excess of anything the viewers possess; the characters live according to simplified but extreme moral and social codes which cause life to be led or lost at an extraordinary pitch. The dramatic organization is arranged to allow rapid presentation of exciting incidents and not to have viewers or readers pausing to consider the plausibility of what is taking place; the dynamism of narrative or scenic develop-ment always has an audience looking ahead to the next incident and not reflecting on what has taken place. *The Jew of Malta* might be the story of a disaffected rich Israeli arms dealer living on an unnamed Mediterranean island controlled by Mafia bosses with Vatican and CIA connections who are running shady deals with an unnamed Arab government. There is even a ·wonderful cameo role for Joan Collins in Katherine, the mother of Mathias.

While I would resist following this direction of suggesting trans-historical similarities between different cultural environments too far, we should not lose sight of the likelihood that the contemporary popularity of *The Jew of Malta* did not rest with the similarities of its 'tragedy' to that of *Hamlet*, let alone *Othello*. Marlowe's drama is not seeking explanations for Barabas which stem from the con-sequences of his social exclusion through race, let alone his interior motivations. The characters are not developed sufficiently to provoke audiences to identify with their dilemmas or feel a deep-seated repugnance over their crimes. In using figures who possess relatively little depth, the play suppresses the potential seriousness of what they perform. Indeed, modern audiences or readers usually experience a comic irony rather than a tragic pathos dominating the play; it emerges as a type of black melodrama. Theatrical excess which maintains the enigma of Faustus or the allurement of Tamburlaine here acts to reduce the significance of the Jew to a stage villain.

Answering Barabas's objections to the sequestration of his wealth, one of the Christian knights points out:

> If your first curse fall heavy on thy head,
> And make thee poor and scorn'd of all the world,
> 'Tis not our fault, but thy inherent sin.

Jew, I. ii. 111–13

The belief that the Jews were cursed as a race was widely accepted in early modern Europe, which even used scriptural authority to demonstrate this 'truth': 'Then answered all the people, and said, His [Christ's] blood be on us, and on our children' (Matt. 27: 25). The Geneva Bible, which was the translation Marlowe was most familiar with, glosses this passage with 'and as they wished, so this curse taketh place to this day'. For contemporary readers there was irony even in entitling the play *The Famous Tragedy of the Rich Jew of Malta*, as the quarto of 1633 does. From sixteenth- or seventeenth-century perspectives, any 'tragedy' in relation to Barabas would rest with the murders he inflicts on Christians; his own decline would demonstrate the justice due his race. Maintenance of Judaism was perceived as a stubborn refusal to witness Christian truth and led to the popular view of the Jew as criminal, a feature which Barabas's words and actions only support. In making it apparent that such 'anti-Christian' behaviour is shared by Roman Catholics as much as it is by the Jew or Turk, the play is subscribing to Protestant ideas of divine election for England. In representing the deceptions, hypocrisies, and immorality of foreigners, the play may be seen as reinforcing the widely disseminated view that the English were a specially chosen people of God in a world of sin. The play also supports the popular xenophobia which was widespread in the London of the 1580s and 1590s.

The Jew of Malta testifies to the cultural difference of Marlowe's world from our own. Literary criticism frequently wishes to emphasize continuity with the past, to demonstrate literary texts as 'speaking' to current readers as they did to previous generations. As a result, aspects of texts or authors which rest uneasily with current social, moral, or political perspectives tend to be 'forgotten' or conveniently transformed through critical interpretation because there is a reluctance to see significant literary achievements articulating ideas which seem repugnant to current perspectives. We should not be hesitant, however, about examining cultural difference. While the presence of many of the play's underlying prejudices continue to haunt the modern world, they now exist against the grain of enlightened tolerance. In contrast, *The Jew of Malta* presents these assumptions as unproblematic certainties, representing them in significantly different perspectives from most modern ones. What is notable, though, is how the play registers an important transformation in dramatic depictions of racial and religious difference within Marlowe's own period, a change which has important implications for subsequent presentations. An older morality tradition saw the demonstration of the evils enacted by different faiths (and the Protestant morality drama of the mid-sixteenth century quickly added Catholics to this group) as indicating the plights and turmoils to which the faithful were subjected. Marlowe's play retains vestiges of this tradition, but he has typically transformed these to secular concerns. *The Jew of Malta* is an entertainment designed to satisfy further the interest in alterity, its attractions and its terrors, we have seen manifested in Marlowe's other plays. The challenge to convention posed by Barabas rests in his meaning as a figure gratifying an audience's desire for amusement not moral edification. The sinister politics of Machiavellianism, the displays of Catholic, Jewish, or Turkish hypocrisies, all become subject to the demands of a new theatre of popular entertainment. As we witness a resurgence of racial and religious persecutions in the late twentieth century, Marlowe's play offers an important illustration of the designs through which racial stereotyping has circulated in Western culture and how perceptions may be moulded by such texts. It remains a challenging document in the largely unexplored but important arena of interactions among serious literature, popular entertainment, and social propaganda.

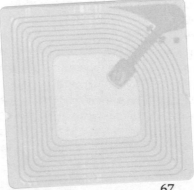

8

Protestant Drama

If the threats posed by racial and religious differences in *The Jew of Malta* are limited by their performance in a foreign location, Marlowe could also use the foreign as a more impinging and unsettling reality. *The Massacre at Paris* is Marlowe's most directly propagandist piece as well as his shortest (at 1,260 lines it is less than half the length of *Edward II*). The play depicts the murders, subterfuges, and other political manœuvrings employed by the ultra-Catholic Guise movement in France during the 1570s and 1580s and especially its notorious massacre of French Protestants on St Bartholomew's Day in 1572. The text of the play which has come down to us is not a good one. It was first printed in an undated edition probably of the early seventeenth century, but it was acted in 1593 and possibly before. We should not blame too many of the play's deficiencies on its transmission, however. It is Marlowe at his most reductive, and exemplifies English popular Protestant sentiment of the period.

The St Bartholomew massacre attained instantaneous legendary status in England as a consummate illustration of Roman Catholic treachery. This is partly because England absorbed large numbers of French Huguenots fleeing their country after the event, but it also indicates wider aspects of the contemporary religious contexts of the two countries. With historical hindsight, it appears to us that by the 1590s France would remain Catholic, England Protestant. This ignores the fears or hopes among many that these directions could be reversed, anxieties or aspirations which were not groundless in either country. At the first performances of *The Massacre at Paris*, the national religions in both countries were imagined as much less secure than it appears from our later day perspectives and the play participates directly in the topicality of these anxieties (the death of Henry III which concludes the play only took place in 1589). *The Massacre* especially manipulates the suspiciousness about foreigners which was widespread in London by illustrating their capacity for destructive deception. For example, fears about a Catholic assassination of Elizabeth would have been enhanced by the friar who murders Henry III justifying the killing of monarchs opposed to the Pope as 'meritorious' and a cause of remission for his sins (*Massacre*, V. iv. 23–8). Legislation in the 1580s which made the practice of Catholicism in England a treasonable offence, coupled with the fears of Spanish invasion, had produced a wave of persecutions of priests entering the country. A climate of suspicion about continental Roman Catholicism was widespread and Marlowe's play wastes no opportunity in demonstrating a scheming diabolical character to the Guise faction's promotion of the Pope's designs against the Protestants, whose virtue is exemplified by the uncomplicated heroism of their leader, Henry of Navarre. Where Guise uses underhand means, Navarre raises an army and wins his right through direct confrontation: 'God we know will always put them down | That lift themselves against the perfect truth' (*Massacre*, IV. iv. 12–13).

One of the features *The Massacre* articulates is the possibility of a joint Anglo-French alliance against the Pope. Navarre expresses his hope that Elizabeth will help him 'beat the papal monarch from our lands' (*Massacre*, IV. iv. 16), while at the conclusion the dying Henry III swears 'to ruinate the wicked Church of Rome' and offers eternal love to Elizabeth, 'Whom God hath bless'd for hating papistry' (*Massacre*, V. v. 56-70). An aspect of much Protestant literature of the Tudor and Stuart periods is its attempts to force English monarchs, perceived as too interested in making peaceful accommodation with continental powers, to follow an active role in leading a northern Protestant crusade against the supposed corrupt Catholic south. Unable to offer direct criticism of the government, such texts try to present an idealized role for the monarch as Protestant hero ready to engage in actions which in reality the State was unwilling to pursue. Marlowe is not thought of as a Protestant writer, but this is an area which should be substantially re-examined. Although, his plays do not share the specific didactic aims of Spenser's *Faerie Queene*, for instance, his constant representations of a Roman Catholic capacity for deception and his drama's recognition that image or language may create illusions whose relation to truth are insecure, propose similarities with a Spenserian cultural perspective formed by the pronounced role of religion in understanding social, political, and all intellectual questions.

The limits of deception are what complicates *The Massacre at Paris* and makes it a more interesting piece than merely a depiction of well-defined Catholic hypocrisy opposing Protestant transparent virtue. The Guise, like Barabas, is a self-confessed dissembler and devilish Machiavellian who combines melodramatic stage villainry with an emblematic illustration of Roman Catholic diabolism. Much more awkward to understand is the role of the French king, Henry III. As we have seen, at the end of the play Henry swears love to England, hatred to Catholicism, and pleasure at the French succession falling to the Protestant Navarre. His last lines are 'Salute the Queen of England in my name | And tell her Henry dies her faithful friend' (*Massacre*, V. v. 116–17). The problem is that Henry's words and actions are often at variance in the play. During the vividly depicted scene of the St Bartholomew Massacre, Henry (as the Duke of Anjou) actively takes part in the killing of Protestants, himself slaying the humanist logician, Ramus. Yet, he denies any such participation a few lines later, claiming to Navarre he has just risen and 'I have done what I could to stay this broil' (*Massacre*, II. i. 73). Anjou is a blatant liar like the Guise – should we be expected to believe him in his supposed death-bed conversion?

Typically, this is left unresolved; but what for us is only uncertainty of interpretation in a play was a much more sinister question for Marlowe's England. The closest Elizabeth came to marriage was with the brother of Henry III, François, who had become Duke of Anjou – a marriage much opposed by militant Protestants in England because of their fears of Catholic influence. The marriage arrangements had long been cancelled by the time of *The Massacre at Paris*, but serious doubts remained about the character of the French and an Anglo-French alliance. In the play, the advent of Henry of Navarre as King of France is portrayed as a promise of Protestant ascendancy; in reality, this was not ultimately the case. While Henry IV initially did allow Protestantism a legal status in France and helped found Protestant universities, he was politically astute enough to spend most of his energies appeasing the Catholic establishment. It is tempting to pursue Marlowe's uncertainty about Henry III to Navarre, but here the dating of the play becomes awkward. If the play was conceived shortly after Henry III's death in 1589, it might be celebrating Navarre genuinely. If it dates from the end of Marlowe's career (and the first recorded performance is 1593), it may ironically reflect Protestant England's growing disillusionment with Henry IV. Whatever the authorial intention, however, it must have been extremely ironic that *The Massacre*'s celebration of Navarre's Protestant fortitude confronted the historical figure's politic conversion to Catholicism in 1593 (with the legendary remark 'Paris is worth a mass'!). *The Massacre at Paris* reminds current readers that Marlowe's drama of scepticism reflects a contemporary cultural climate frequently uneasy about the security of a social and spiritual fabric seen as threatened by forces real and imagined, both within the nation and without.

Whether it was prompted by commercial opportunity or ideological conviction, *The Massacre at Paris* demonstrates that Marlowe employed his dramatic art not only to challenge cultural norms and conventions but to reinforce local biases and sectarian perceptions. *The Massacre* is a fascinating cultural document whose implications for the commercial drama and its relation to English Protestantism have yet to be explored with any thoroughness. The play poses important questions about the role of the stage in reflecting or promoting ideology and for the relations of a propagandist drama to various political factions within the City of London and at the English court. It is also true that *The Massacre* is Marlowe's least successful piece of drama, functioning almost entirely through reductive stereotypes and relying on a continuous display of murder and assassination to maintain interest. When the events it depicts were topical it probably generated considerable excitement but it is understandably the least of Marlowe's plays from a modern perspective.

Interestingly, Marlowe employed many of the same structures in what is his most sophisticated play, *Edward II* – a drama which also incorporates many of the preoccupations of Marlowe's other plays: attempted re-arrangement of the social fabric, figures apparently victims of their passions, uncertainty about what governs human affairs. Unlike the other plays, though, *Edward II* is set in England. Significantly, it combines displays of sexuality – notably homosexuality – with a perspective which is largely Protestant in its implications (a pairing which at first sight might seem somewhat incompatible!). The play presents a good case for viewing Marlowe as a Protestant dramatist in a larger sense than is demonstrated in his distinctly propagandist *The Massacre at Paris*. It also testifies to the difficulties we face in comprehending the different cultural categories and structures Elizabethan England employed to figure experience.

The idea of a Protestant drama in late Tudor and Stuart England is one which we are becoming ever more familiar with after the important work of the late Margot Heinemann on Middleton or, more recently, Julia Gaspar on Dekker. It is not a drama of easily observed theology; nor is it the logical development of the Protestant morality plays which found favour with the early English Reformers. A supernatural organization of the world which saw constant attempts by the forces of the Antichrist to challenge the godly and which believed the majority of humanity necessarily damned, however, found cultural expression in plays which explore the implications of these conditions. In particular, this drama proposes that characters discover their actions linked to patterns which seem determined, exhibiting a fatalism which hints at inevitabilities in humanity's fallen condition. Revelations of identities are performed, but these uncoverings of character – even in apparent discoveries of self – reveal that identity is outside self-control.

The Protestant Reformer, John Calvin, spoke of theatres of the world where humanity may be stunned, dazzled, and blinded by the world's allurements which falsely promise grace and sweetness. It is this startling quality to the world, where what first seems revealed is actually deceptive – a reality whose nature is never entirely clear – which Marlowe explores uncompromisingly in *Edward II*. The play is a study in deceptions intimately combined with sexuality, proposing no easy resolutions to the dilemmas it poses. It posits an inescapable pattern to events, offering no ready solace to its audiences. More than any other Marlowe play, *Edward II* demonstrates an unknowable world where all forms of relationships are insecure and uncertain, a drama which questions the audience's ability to determine what is lawful, moral, natural. This insecurity for the play's witnesses arises because many of the characters themselves seem to fail to comprehend the nature of their allotted roles. In a cultural environment which widely accepted predestination for humanity, a considerable anxiety was that belief in salvation or damnation (particularly the former) might be self-deluding. Even those who appear among the righteous may find themselves among the fallen, their apparent revulsion against the illicit no more than an indication of the desires proper to their condition which they refuse to credit. In exploring the nature of treason, *Edward II* represents such underlying supernatural currents within events of political intrigue which dramatically culminate in a death combining sex and violence.

Our critical practice with Renaissance literature commonly operates on assumptions that early modern people experienced and wrote about sexuality according to cultural sensibilities similar to our own. But, during Marlowe's time, categories for defining sexualities were organized in importantly different ways from modern ones. We are only beginning to appreciate that current cultural constructions of sexual orientations (how practices are identified and assimilated into society's understanding) do not easily mesh with representations of sex in Renaissance texts. John Donne, for example, obviously imagines women as his lovers in a large number of his lyrics; yet he chastises his *alter ego* in *Satyre I* with loving both 'plumpe muddy whore' and 'prostitute boy'. Certainly, strong arguments can be advanced for reading a number of Donne's lyrics, including the well-known 'The Good Morrow', as addressing another man and celebrating same-sex passions.

During the late sixteenth century, it seems likely that men could engage in sexual acts with other men without thinking of themselves as homosexual in the ways that this is currently conceived. Shakespeare presents Oberon in *A Midsummer Night's Dream* quarrelling with his wife Titania both because she accuses him of philandering with a girl and because he desires a boy whom she has under her protection – his sexual appetite readily and unashamedly crosses gender divisions! And, if the actualities of early modern sexuality are frequently difficult to construe, the possible meanings of representations of sexuality in the drama also raise complex problems of interpretation. Plays were not seeking to record the cultural meanings of sexuality in authentic manners, as though anticipating the needs of current historians for an archive of information on gender and its effects. How the drama represented sexuality reflects many things – including generic choice, specific historical circumstances, ideological choices, and responses to the wishes of audiences to witness exaggerations and differences from the everyday.

As we have seen, Marlowe uses a language of erotic fascination to depict Theridamas' and Zenocrate's compelling fascination with Tamburlaine, or he lets Faustus imagine himself in both male and female guises in experiencing sexual arousal with Helen of Troy. In *Edward II* sexuality plays a central role in Marlowe's portrayal of an uncertain world – one where even the most intimate relationships are open to manipulation and treachery. To attempt to understand

Marlowe's use of sexuality in this play, however, requires a modern reader to fathom cultural preconceptions which are not easily analogous with present ones. In particular, categorization of the differences between the illicit, the questionable, and the permissible in the play's representation of sexuality requires some understanding of the different cultural mentality of Marlowe's world.

The death of Edward is a reversal of the play's opening where Gaveston's promises of sensual excess as his means of maintaining Edward's affection provokes the barons' disgust supposedly because of the state's declining integrity. Our first encounter with Gaveston, his lengthy description of the delights with which he will control the king (cited in Chapter 1), creates suspicions. His ornamented eloquence makes it clear he uses a language of flattery and is a dissembler. The play initially organizes itself to present Gaveston and Edward as decadent rioters, the barons as defenders of a status quo.

The barons object to Gaveston's influence on Edward on three main accounts: the exchequer is being drained, a foreign and decadent aesthetic is being promoted in the English court, and, most significantly, Gaveston is basely born and has no right to gain high office. In an exchange between the Mortimers after Gaveston, Edward, and the nobles have been momentarily reconciled, it is proposed that it is not sexual frolics between Edward and Gaveston which are troublesome. Mortimer senior argues that the king is by nature 'mild and calm' and should be allowed to dote on Gaveston as his minion, citing a number of classical precedents:

> Then let his grace, whose youth is flexible,
> And promiseth as much as we can wish,
> Freely enjoy that vain light-headed earl,
> For riper years will wean him from such toys.

> *Ed. II*, I. iv. 400–3.

The senior Mortimer marks out a socially acceptable way of viewing Gaveston's and Edward's relationship, one in which sexuality is not a corrupting influence but an amusement. Edward's actions, which might be viewed as revealing effeminate indecision and emotional dotage in other contexts, are ascribed to his youth. The promise of Edward which Mortimer indicates is ambiguous, but it suggests that the barons do not automatically view Gaveston's and Edward's relationship as unmanning, and, to Elizabethan understanding, corrupting of Edward.

Mortimer junior agrees that Edward's 'wanton humour' is not troublesome. His dismay at the relations between Gaveston and Edward, he claims, is motivated by national needs mixed with a repulsion at Gaveston's importation of foreign courtly behaviour, particularly because Gaveston is of lowly origins. The barons' difficulty with Gaveston is a fear that the state's structures of power are being re-arranged. Gaveston's use of shows and foreign manners to gain control of the king is against a courtliness based on landed might and inherited privilege. Gaveston's imported courtliness is one the younger Mortimer has no tolerance of:

> I scorn, that one so basely born
> Should by his sovereign's favour grow so pert,
> And riot it with the treasure of the realm,
> While soldiers mutiny for want of pay.
> He wears a lord's revenue on his back,
> And, Midas-like, he jets it in the court
>
> Whiles other walk below, the king and he
> From out a window laugh at such as we,
> And flout our train, and jest at our attire
> Uncle, 'tis this that makes me impatient.

Ed. II, I. iv. 405–10, 418–21

As we have seen, questions of foreignness are important for Marlowe's drama and their significance for Protestantism is well illustrated by *The Massacre at Paris*. Despite its English setting the foreign is crucial, too, in *Edward II* and its role helps illuminate the play's Protestant concerns. The drama opens with Gaveston dismissing a poor soldier to the hospitals he claims exist for such as him. Mortimer's anger that soldiers mutiny for lack of pay while Gaveston lives extravagantly redirects out attention to this theme. The problem of disbanded soldiers in the London of the early 1590s was an acute one in a period of high unemployment. They were feared as masterless and potentially criminal but also represented an embarrassment to the authorities who were charged with neglecting those who had fought in Protestant causes against Spain. At the same time, the late 1580s and early 1590s had produced huge tensions over immigration in London, where aliens were frequently blamed for economic difficulties and the apprentices constantly threatened violence against foreigners as a means of having the authorities address their grievances. Given the xenophobia which existed in London, Gaveston's and Edward's desires for foreign manifestations of sensuality and their extravagances which lead to reported economic wants in the country would not have been calculated to endear them to London audiences of the mid-1590s. Mortimer's defence of native plainness appears patriotic in this context.

Sexuality plays an important part in the construction of the foreign, because illicit sexuality, notably sodomy, was commonly perceived as more prevalent in ungodly places. In English law of this period, sodomy was an unnatural practice punishable by death; yet sodomy does not seem to have been viewed as widespread or culturally subversive when it was clearly only associated with a sexual act. As Bruce Smith notes in his important book, *Homosexual Desire in Shakespeare's England*, in the forty-five years of Elizabeth's and James's reigns there are records of only six men being indicted simply on the charge of sodomy in the home counties and only one conviction. In contrast, sodomy was a common accompanying charge for Roman Catholics or others arrested and condemned for anti-state activities. The Henrician convention of seeing sodomy in terms of heresy seems to have remained largely in place. This was certainly the context of sodomy in early Protestant drama. In John Bale's *Three Laws* (c. 1635), for instance, the figure of Sodom announces: 'In Rome to me they fall | Both Bishop and Cardinal| Monk, friar, priest and all.' Sodomy was socially feared because it indicated the intrusion of diabolical treachery into the midst of the godly.

Importantly, therefore, sodomy does not appear to have been automatically equated with other forms of homosocial and even homosexual behaviour. Where we commonly classify all forms of same-sex activities as registering sexual desires, this does not appear to have been the case with the early modern period. Sharing a bed with another man to gain privacy for study and conversation could be presented as healthy male friendship – the humanist Roger Ascham's account in his *The Scholemaster* (1570) of reading through Cicero's tract on friendship, *De amicitia*, while in bed with a young man named John Whitney is a famous instance. Ascham develops a motif of seclusion from the world for master and pupil, their privacy signalling their innocence from worldly vice.

In contrast, where accusations of sodomy were made against those involved in political or religious treasons, the intimacies of the accused indicated his corruption of all social norms. It was felt to be necessary to display condemned traitors as thoroughly infectious to the state in every aspect of their life-styles. As a result, sexual practices were readily equated with religious questions and, significantly, evidence of illicit sexual practice did not need to be actually proven among those found guilty of treachery or heresy. Establishing guilt in political actions confirmed illicit sexuality and allowed the popular imagination to develop an expectation of treachery being accompanied by sexual corruptions. The drama's representations of proscribed sexual practices as signifying ungodly activities against the State were well supported in pulpit and law court.

Edward dies in the play through a terrible parody of sodomy. A red-hot spit is pushed up his rectum while he is pressed between a feather bed and a table, the actions being devised so that no marks will appear on his body. Given Edward's relation with Gaveston, there might be a temptation to witness this terrible death as having a type of biblical propriety about it, a consummation of unnatural desires and a punishment for them. This is, however, to ignore the reversals which take place in the play. At the dramatization of Edward's death, the entire weight of illicit sexuality has shifted from the king and his minions to Mortimer and Isabella. In our discovery of Mortimer's and Isabella's rebellious adultery against husband, monarchy, and State, there is the revelation of their deceptiveness. The positions of honour, of loyalty, of social order they claimed to uphold at the play's start are revealed to have been false, part of their design to gain control of the realm. At the moment of Edward's death, it is Mortimer and Isabella who have demonstrated themselves as the usurpers of the kingdom, the true abusers of social, political, and moral orders.

It is Mortimer who commands the death of Edward and it is he who is ultimately responsible for the murderous act of sodomy against him. There is a wonderful and yet unsettling irony here. Mortimer does not know how Edward will die. His orders are performed by the hired murderer Lightborn, who reveals that his devious methods of killing people were learnt in Naples, showing Mortimer as an importer of ugly foreign practices into the realm. When Mortimer asks him what his method in killing Edward will be, Lightborn refuses to divulge his trade secrets. Yet Mortimer's unknown and grisly sodomy on Edward is the culmination of his unnatural usurpation of the kingdom. The ostensibly native patriot, fiercely desirous to maintain the status quo and dismissive of Gaveston's baseness and foreignness, becomes the figure, far more than any other in the play, who assumes a role above his station and does so through embracing both unnatural sex and the alien. Although unplanned, the act of murderous ritualized sodomy against Edward is the logical conclusion of Mortimer's designs. Mortimer, the fiercest denouncer of Gaveston, is revealed as perpetrating the deceptions, corruptions, and sodomies he claimed to be passionately opposed to.

Mortimer's position in seeking power would be untenable without Isabella. As the sister to the King of France, Isabella is a foreigner, though she appears to attempt reconciliation among the English in the early part of the play. She constantly claims that accusations of infidelities made against her are false and the early scenes appear to support her eloquent testimony of love for Edward. By the play's conclusion, Isabella's word has been wholly discredited, considerable energy being expended in demonstrating her capacities for deception. In the last act, in the space of a hundred lines, Isabella offers a variety of different faces to different figures. She swears her affection for Mortimer and proposes he should do against Edward 'what thou wilt, | And I myself will willingly subscribe' (*Ed. II*, V. ii. 19–20); she then publicly grieves over Edward's condition; next she rejoices at the news of Edward's resignation of the crown; then she expresses her desire to have Edward dead; she then goes on to announce that she is labouring to ease Edward's grief and gain his freedom; and finally she states her sorrow at the news of Edward's resignation. In case the audience misses the duplicity in her protean dispositions, Mortimer and Edmund have asides which point out her dissembling. As Edmund, the duped brother of Edward, realizes: 'Mortimer | And Isabel do kiss, while they conspire. | And yet she bears a face of love' (*Ed. II*, IV. v. 21–3).

Isabella's attempts to deceive through feigning love for Edward reappear even in the play's closing moments as she attempts to save herself. Given this ability to assume false roles and present herself as a dutiful wife when in fact adulterously involved with Mortimer, Edward's early dismissals of Isabella must be open to reappraisal by the play's conclusion. What seemed unwarranted and hostile rejections gain political credibility.

Edward II, therefore, is calculated to frustrate attempts to categorize it as a play about the ruler's need to keep a tight check on his appetites if proper balances in the nation's orders are to be maintained. Actions and language, and the gap between them, reveal deception and counter-deceptions. Edward's passionate espousal of Gaveston as the man who 'loves me more than all the world' (*Ed. II*, I. iv. 77), which at first appears based simply on emotional attraction, increasingly takes on political overtones. Gaveston and his replacements Spencer and Baldock remain loyal to Edward, even though their loyalties have been in some way purchased. The appearance on the stage of Old Spencer marks a significant shift in the play. Old Spencer and his band of quintessential English soldiery – bowmen, pikes, brown bills, and targetters – 'Sworn to defend King Edward's royal right', undermine the barons' claims to represent the nation (*Ed. II*, III. ii. 36–8). Old Spencer's and his men's loyalties to Edward come from the king's advancement of his son: they are 'bound to your highness everlastingly | For favours done, in him, unto us all' (*Ed. II*, III. ii. 41–2). This is precisely the traditional organization of power vested in the monarch's granting of licences and favours which the barons claim exclusively for themselves. The play increasingly recasts Edward's actions so as to make them seem designs to assert his own monarchical power by refiguring existing orders, and less the consequences of uncontrollable emotions. Importantly, the historian Mervyn James in *Society, Politics and Culture* has shown how such traditional constructions of duties and allegiances were under pressure in late-sixteenth-century England; while Alan Bray's 'Homosexuality and the Signs of Male Friendship in Elizabethan England' has demonstrated how the rhetoric of friendship points to 'that network of influential patrons, of their clients and suitors and friends at court which were [the] subtle bonds of early modern society'. With the arrival of Old Spencer, Edward's faction becomes popularist, native, and decisive in action while the queen and the barons now appear usurpatious, self-seeking, and deceptive.

Sexuality in the play is, thus, intimately tied to political manœuvring, treachery, and the uncovering of deception against the nation. This illustrates once more Marlovian drama's understanding about the function of characters as vehicles for actions, not the development of complex psychologies. *Edward II*'s portrayal of sexualities is unconcerned with sex as a demonstration of individual subjectivities: sexuality here does not propose the illusion of realism. To suggest Edward is fickle, or has some pathological dependency on his minions because he seems to forget Gaveston immediately and transfers his affections to the younger Spencer, is to seek for a psychological causation alien to these figures. It is crucial to the play's revelation of Mortimer that he is the source of murderous sodomy, but it is also significant that he is unaware of the ritualized buggery for which he is responsible. The action eschews attempts to imagine Mortimer as homophobic because of his own repressed homosexuality. Instead, it demonstrates a fatalistic irony in his perpetration of what he ostensibly stands opposed to – a telling representation of Mortimer's unnatural rebellion against his sovereign. *Edward II* manœuvres its audience initially to imagine deviance where it was not and then finally exposes it to be located among those who claim to seek to repress it.

In our wish to indicate continuities between early modern writing and our own cultural environment, we too often allow teleologies into our critical practices. While we may recognize early modern differences, there is a frequent critical slippage in which current cultural frameworks are too readily used to make sense of Renaissance writing. Although we have come to recognize that sexuality is a human construct – that how sex is imagined, how it operates in societies, what is considered natural or deviant, alter according to time and place – there is a tendency to seek out aspects of texts which appear to offer some stirrings of sexuality as subjectivity, early manifestations of the twentieth century's conviction that sexuality is a point of departure for a discovery of personal identity. Psychoanalytic theory, which, especially in Freudianism, tends to ignore particularities of culture difference, has helped to provide frameworks for analysis which oppose the view that sexuality is accountable to history.

Edward II is concerned with dramatizing individual passions in order to illustrate larger social and political machinations, a use of characters as complex types rather than complex personalities. The queen's infidelities signal her deceptive and dangerous qualities as a foreigner in the English state subtly working for its overthrow. Her sexual unfaithfulness to Edward is a telling indication of her lack of loyalty and obedience, a sign of her treachery, whose political manifestation is finally confirmed. Although many Renaissance dramas represent women as emotionally ungovernable, happy to jump into bed at the first seductive offer, Isabella's organized dissembling is much more careful and diabolical. The play shares a widespread Renaissance cultural misogyny in its proposal that a woman may be the most dangerous corrupter because the most able dissembler, but Isabella's foreignness is as significant as her gender. Her French origins create an important link with *The Massacre at Paris* and her capacity for subterfuge shares that play's proposal that deceptiveness is virtually a French national characteristic. Marlowe creates a balanced reversal in *Edward II* so that Gaveston, initially the apparent seducer of the State through his exotic enticements of Edward, dies more innocent of treachery against the king than others, while Isabella, initially the apparent victim, ends as the play's greatest criminal.

In many respects *Edward II* is Marlowe's most difficult play because it resolves so little. The structure through which it reveals deceptions at all levels and among virtually all characters is carefully calculated to undermine an audience's capacity to interpret actions, leaving confusion – an insecurity with existing categories, including literary generic patterns, through which events are normally understood. The play certainly does not present cases of villains becoming heroes and heroes villains. In revealing Mortimer's and Isabella's usurpatious and illicit sex, Gaveston's manipulation of Edward's emotions may appear far less treacherous, but it is not celebrated. Instead, the play seems concerned to demonstrate the depths of treachery – deceptions I see tied to Protestant anxieties about counterfeits both abroad and at home, and which reflect the potentials for self-delusion apparent in a cultural framework which asserted predestination. If *Edward II* has a message, it is clearly not to accept appearances and words at face value; but the play presents a bleak vision of human ability to know, or control, self and the world. Mortimer's final speech proposes that fate is linked to a secular wheel of fortune, but this, too, is an ironical self-assessment of a figure who imagines he rose to the top of Fortune's wheel at the very moment he was ordering a murderous sodomy which completed his treachery against all order. Mortimer's imagined high point can be just as easily seen as his lowest one; he is self-deluded, a victim, as it were, of Calvin's theatre of the world which dazzles and blinds humanity with the allurement of worldly success.

Early in the play, after the nobles have forced the banishment of Gaveston, Edward launches a diatribe against Rome, a force he perceives underlying the nobles' conspiracy against him: 'Why should a king be subject to a priest? | Proud Rome, that hatchest such imperial grooms' (*Ed. II*, I. iv. 97–8). Here and elsewhere, Edward depicts himself as trying to maintain English national integrity against the Roman Church's meddling, using a language and imagery appropriate to a late-sixteenth-century Protestant. This attempt to dramatize English kings or nobles from the past as proto-Protestants is commonly found in English history plays; in *Edward II* the motif reinforces Marlowe's presentation of Roman Catholicism as the diabolical foreign, capable of infecting the English State. Edward's gruesome death on the stage, a spectacle of cruelty virtually unsurpassed in English theatre, was also one of the first visual stagings of the murder of an English monarch. It is a grim representation of the failure of Edward to curtail the nobles who support the foreign queen, the power of the Pope, and, perhaps even the supernatural evil imagined lurking underneath. As we might expect from Marlowe, *Edward II* is not a Protestant morality play which insists upon the triumph of the righteous but an uncomfortable spectacle which powerfully suggests that in the continuing struggle between 'the old foe' and the godly even an English monarch may become a victim.

The conclusion of *Doctor Faustus* – as we witness Faustus being taken off to hell and (in the B version of the play) see his dismembered limbs – has similarities with the end of *Edward II*. As we have examined, however, the comic parodies in *Faustus* condition the tragic potentials of its end. The terribleness of Edward's death is not hindered by any comic trickery. In witnessing a ritual sodomy in the murder of an English king in the mire of a dungeon and the apparent triumph of the two arch-deceivers, it is hard to resist the sense that England can become a type of hell. Although the play formally ends with Edward III gaining control of the crown, this potential for the future does not interfere with the tragedy of the dramatized present. The play is Marlowe's bleakest. If *Edward II* was Marlowe's last play, as it is often assumed to be, it suggests that Marlowe's scepticism moved from an excitement about the challenge to convention possible in a figure such as Tamburlaine to a darker vision about the potentials for treason. As Marlowe's drama moves closer to England in *The Massacre at Paris* and *Edward II*, the unresolved quality of his plays, which helped generate a 'wonder of discontinuity' in their depictions of an exotic, remote alterity, becomes more threatening. In considering England, Marlowe's drama suggests that the demands of an entertainment offering the allurement of rank and wealth give way to a theatre provoking uneasy speculations about the condition of the realm.

Select Bibliography

WORKS BY CHRISTOPHER MARLOWE

The Complete Works of Christopher Marlowe, ed. F. Bowers, 2 vols. (2nd edn., Cambridge, 1981). The standard scholarly old-spelling edition.

The Works of Christopher Marlowe, ed. C. F. Tucker Brooke (Oxford, 1910; repr. 1969). Excellent old-spelling edition, remains invaluable.

The Complete Works of Christopher Marlowe, i. *Translations*, ed. R. Gill (Oxford, 1987); ii. *Dr Faustus*, ed. R. Gill (Oxford, 1990); iii. *Edward II*, ed. R. Rowland (Oxford, forthcoming, 1994).

Christopher Marlowe: The Complete Plays, ed. J. B. Steane (Harmondsworth, 1969, repr. 1991). Modern-spelling student edition.

Doctor Faustus: A 1604 version edition, ed. M. Keefer (Peterborough, Ont., 1991). Containing an excellent introduction and very full commentary.

The Revel series's editions of Marlowe plays are the best scholarly single-play editions containing important textual and critical annotation:

Dido, Queen of Carthage and *The Massacre at Paris*, ed. H. J. Oliver (London, 1968).

The Poems, ed. M. Maclure (London, 1968).

The Jew of Malta, ed. N. W. Bawcutt (Manchester, 1978).

Tamburlaine the Great, ed. J. S. Cunningham (Manchester, 1981).

Doctor Faustus A- and B-texts (1604, 1616), ed. D. Bevington and E. Rasmussen (Manchester, 1993).

Edward II, ed. C. R. Forker (Manchester, 1994).

BIOGRAPHICAL STUDIES

Bakeless, J., *The Tragical History of Christopher Marlowe*, 2 vols. (1942, repr. Hamden, Conn., 1964). The most reliable and complete guide to Marlowe's life.

Boas, F. S., *Christopher Marlowe: A Biographical and Critical Study* (Oxford, 1940, rev. edn., 1953).

Nicholl, C., *The Reckoning* (London, 1992). Portrays Marlowe's relation with the secret service; well documented but overly speculative.

Urry, W., *Christopher Marlowe and Canterbury*, ed. A. Butcher (London, 1988). An impressive reconstruction of the social milieu of Marlowe's early years.

CRITICAL STUDIES

Cartelli, T., *Marlowe, Shakespeare, and the Economy of Theatrical Experience* (Philadelphia, Pa., 1991). Important book which relates text to performance and tries to imagine the conditions of Marlowe's original theatre.

Dollimore, J., *Radical Tragedy: Religion, Ideology and Power in the Drama of Shakespeare and his Contemporaries* (2nd edn., Hemel Hempstead, 1989). Stimulating consideration of subversion and transgression in *Doctor Faustus*.

Empson, W., *Faustus and the Censor: The English Faust-book and Marlowe's Doctor Faustus*, ed. J. H. Jones (Oxford, 1987). Ultimately an unsustainable thesis about censorship and the two texts of the play, but always readable and provocative.

Friendereich, K., Gill, R., and Kuriyama, C. B. (eds.), *'A Poet and Filthy Playmaker': New Essays on Christopher Marlowe* (New York, 1988). Solid scholarship by leading Marlowe critics but not a particularly exciting collection.

Goldberg, J., *Sodometries: Renaissance Texts, Modern Sexualities* (Stanford, Calif., 1992). Has a provocative account of gay sexuality and the conventions of all male acting in Elizabethan performances of Marlowe's plays.

Greenblatt, S., *Renaissance Self-Fashioning: From More to Shakespeare* (Chicago and London, 1980). 'Marlowe and the Will to Absolute Play' is a classic new historicist study, illuminating and lively.

—*Learning to Curse: Essays in Early Modern Culture* (New York and London, 1990). 'Marlowe, Marx and Anti-Semitism' addresses the racial and allied questions for cultural interpretation raised by *The Jew of Malta*.

Hattaway, M., *Elizabethan Popular Theatre: Plays in Performance* (London, 1982). Interesting considerations of *Faustus* and *Edward II* as manifestations of the new commercial theatre.

Keach, W., *Elizabethan Erotic Narratives: Irony and Pathos in the Ovidian Poetry of Shakespeare, Marlowe and their Contemporaries* (Hassocks, 1977). A very good introduction to *Hero and Leander*.

Kelsall, M., *Christopher Marlowe* (Leiden, 1981). A judicious and interesting consideration of the poems, plays, and the Marlowe 'phenomenon'.

Kernan, A. B. (ed.), *Two Renaissance Mythmakers: Christopher Marlowe and Ben Jonson* (Baltimore and London, 1977). Excellent collection of essays; see particularly Marjorie Garber on Marlowe's use of spatial effects.

Leech, C. (ed.), *Marlowe: A Collection of Critical Essays* (Twentieth Century Views Series; Englewood Cliffs, NJ, 1964). Although much of this material seems dated it reflects the influential intellectual and aesthetic preoccupations of, largely, American New Criticism.

Levin, H., *The Overreacher* (London, 1954). A classic thesis arguing that Marlowe's characters exceed permitted norms and therefore decline.

Maclure, M. (ed.), *Marlowe: The Critical Heritage: 1588–1896* (London, 1979).

Rhodes, N., *The Power of Eloquence and English Renaissance Literature* (Hemel Hempstead, 1992). A lucid, well-informed introduction to rhetoric and its impact on Marlowe's language.

Sales, R., *Christopher Marlowe* (Basingstoke, 1991). Concerned to represent Elizabethan social mentalities as exhibited in the plays.

Sanders, W., *The Dramatist and the Received Idea: Studies in the Plays of Marlowe and Shakespeare* (Cambridge, 1968). Moral criticism favouring Shakespeare over Marlowe. A classic example of the unease Marlowe's plays have generated among liberal humanist critics desiring literature to address supposedly timeless human values.

Shepherd, S., *Marlowe and the Politics of Elizabethan Theatre* (Brighton, 1986). Ambitious book examining the drama's interventions in contemporary social and political issues. Very good on Marlowe in relation to other Renaissance drama.

Sinfield, A., *Faultlines: Cultural Materialism and the Politics of Dissident Reading* (Oxford, 1992). Wide-ranging study containing a lively piece on the politics of religion and *Doctor Faustus*.

Weil, J. F. R., *Christopher Marlowe: Merlin's Prophet* (Cambridge, 1977). The best study of Marlowe and Renaissance occult philosophy.

OTHER READING

Bhabha, H. K., 'The Commitment to Theory', *New Formations*, 5 (1988), 5–23.

Bakhtin, M., *Rabelais and his World*, trans. H. Iswolsky (Boston, Mass., 1968).

Belsey, C., *The Subject of Tragedy: Identity and Difference in Renaissance Drama* (London, 1985).

Bray, A., 'Homosexuality and the Signs of Male Friendship in Elizabethan England', *History Workshop Journal*, 29 (1990), 1–19.

Diehl, H., 'Dazzling Theatre: Renaissance Drama in the Age of Reform', *Journal of Medieval and Renaissance Studies*, 22 (1992), 211–36.

Foucault, M., 'What is an Author?', trans. J. V. Harai, in D. Lodge (ed.), *Modern Criticism and Theory: A Reader* (Harlow, 1988).

Gaspar, J., *The Dragon and the Dove: The Plays of Thomas Dekker* (Oxford, 1990).

Greenblatt, S., *Marvellous Possessions: The Wonder of the New World* (Oxford, 1991).

Heinemann, M., *Puritanism and Theatre: Thomas Middleton and Opposition Drama under the Early Stuarts* (Cambridge, 1980).

Hutson, L., *Thomas Nashe in Context* (Oxford, 1989).

James, M., *Society, Politics and Culture: Studies in Early Modern England* (Cambridge, 1986).

Mullaney, S., *The Place of the Stage: License, Play, and Power in Renaissance England* (Chicago and London, 1988).

Otis, B., *Virgil: A Study in Civilized Poetry* (London, 1963).

Smith, B. R., *Homosexual Desire in Shakespeare's England: A Cultural Poetics* (Chicago and London, 1991).

Whitfield White, P., *Theatre and Reformation: Protestantism, Patronage and Playing in Tudor England* (Cambridge, 1993).

Index